The Leadership Lectures

Lectures on leadership prepared for health care leaders, managers, and supervisors.

Dale S. Benson, MD, CPE, FAAPL

Fellow, American Association for Physician Leadership
Director, Leadership Development Institute
AltaMed Health Services
Los Angeles, California

Cover design by Julia Zollman Wickes

Copyright 2017 by the Author

This book was printed by CreateSpace. The author retains sole copyright on his contributions to this book.

First edition, September 2014. Second edition, December 2017.

Dedication

Being a firm believer in the notion that everyone has something to teach you, I wish to dedicate this book to the many health care professionals who have unknowingly mentored me over the years. I have never had an official mentor, but have been fortunate to have worked alongside a number of giants in their respective fields. The secret is to look for peers whom you admire, figure out what it is that you admire about them, and then learn from watching them. As Yogi Berra may or may not have said, "You can observe a lot by just watching." You giants don't know who you are, but I do, and I thank you immensely for all that I have learned by watching you in action.

Dale Benson
December 2017

Table of Contents

Introduction to the Leadership Lectures 1

Chapter One

Leadership and the Rediscovery of Fire.. **6**

Chapter Two

The Five Fundamental Tasks of a Transformational Leader......... **24**

Chapter Three

Building the Mental Model for Leadership.................................... **42**

Chapter Four

Crafting Your Personal Leadership Philosophy **57**

Chapter Five

Leading Beyond the Bottom Line **67**

Chapter Six

Embracing Change: Four Critical Concepts **91**

Chapter Seven

How To Be Effective When There Is No Time............................. **108**

Chapter Eight

Twelve Tips for Leadership Effectiveness.................................... **127**

Chapter Nine

Connecting the Threads **143**

Chapter Ten

Step Into It!.. **155**

Chapter Eleven

Eight Rules for a Fulfilling Career *163*

Chapter Twelve

Your Legacy Awaits *177*

Bibliography.. *181*

About the Author *188*

Leadership

*Leaders are called to stand in that lonely place
between the no longer and the not yet
and intentionally make decisions
that will bind, forge, move
and create history.*

*We are not called to be popular,
we are not called to be safe,
we are not called to follow,
we are the ones called to take risks,
we are the ones called to change attitudes;
to risk displeasures,
we are the ones called to gamble our lives
for a better world.*

Mary Lou Andersen
Former Deputy Director
Bureau of Primary Health Care
April 1970

Introduction to the Leadership Lectures

The craft of leadership has always been intriguing to me. From president of our church youth group to president of our condo homeowners' association 50 years later, my ideas about leadership have constantly been challenged and refined. In college I was elected president of our freshman class, and then, in my senior year, president of the Student Association. As fate would have it, after completing medical school and family practice training, I stepped into a leadership role in our Indianapolis community health centers on day one as the designated director of a six-person staff in two storefront clinics. Thirty years later I was still there, now CEO of a community health center network with hundreds of employees and thousands of patients. We called the organization HealthNet.

During the later years in Indianapolis, I became active in the American College of Physician Executives (now the American Association for Physician Leadership), an organization of more than 10,000 physicians with management and executive responsibilities in health care organizations. I chaired the task force on quality, was elected to the Board, and in 1998 began a term as president of the College. I also served a term as chair of the Certifying Commission in Medical Management.

After 30 years at HealthNet in Indianapolis, I moved on to Chicago to accept a Vice President position in the Mercy Health System. From there I went to AltaMed Health Services in Los Angeles, this time as Vice President of Innovation, Quality, and Practice Management. AltaMed has delivered quality care to the underserved communities of Southern California for nearly 50 years.

Introduction to the Leadership Lectures

AltaMed was, and still is, a large community health center network with a primary mission to Latino, multi-ethnic and underserved communities in Southern California. As of 2014, AltaMed was the largest independent Federally Qualified Community Health Center in the U.S., delivering more than 930,000 annual patient visits through its 43 service delivery sites in Los Angeles and Orange Counties.

While at AltaMed, halfway through the first decade of the 2000's it occurred to me that the time had come to pass on some of the many lessons I had learned over the years relating to leadership. And so, with the support of our CEO, Castulo de la Rocha, I helped to inaugurate the AltaMed Leadership Development Institute. Out of its 800 (at the time) employees, 100 leaders, managers and supervisors signed up to become members of the Leadership Institute. The 100 included the CEO, the Vice Presidents, nearly all managers and department heads, and many of the supervisors. The Institute was designed to impact leadership at all levels.

The AltaMed Leadership Development Institute was structured so that it offered one three-hour session each month. The first hour consisted of a lecture on leadership. The second was devoted to discussion of a relevant leadership book. The third of the three hours focused on practical management issues.

Many, but not all, of the leadership lectures were presented by myself, as Director of the Institute. We brought in other outside leadership experts to provide additional perspectives - leaders such as Air Force Two Star General Leonard Randolph, who presented "The Nuts and Bolts of Leadership." Other outside expert presentations included "Six Life Lessons in Leadership," shared by Charles B. Van Vorst, former CEO of four major health care systems; "Creating a Personal Leadership Development Plan," by Marilyn Soulsburg, former Director of Leadership Development for the Internal Revenue Service; and "Five Star/Five Diamond Customer Service," by Drew Vactor, former owner and manager of Arizona's first five star/five diamond restaurant. We also brought in leadership consultant Les Wallace for two sessions: "Managing Change," and "Leadership and the Mentoring Process."

The Leadership Lectures

I prepared a number of 45-50 minute lectures on subjects relating to leadership - each one building on the preceding lectures. Because it was so important to me to communicate clearly, I wrote out in advance nearly every word of each lecture. I have selected a dozen of these lectures for this book.

Of course, the lectures were prepared for the leadership and management staff of AltaMed. In that sense they are not generic. Yet, I have made the decision not to delete specific references to AltaMed in Los Angeles (nor HealthNet in Indianapolis). These lectures are indeed "up close and personal." But the principles, ideas and techniques are relevant to any health care organization of any size.

In studying these lectures, you will encounter examples and challenges noted as applicable to AltaMed in Los Angeles and HealthNet in Indianapolis. Substitute the name of your organization. It is quite likely that what you are reading will sound very familiar.

Please note that these chapters are not essays. They were written as lectures. You will find many sentence fragments; sentence fragments are not so good in an essay, but they are essential for making and reinforcing points in a lecture. The bibliography for all of the footnotes can be found organized by chapter at the end of the book.

You will find that these lectures move from the conceptual to the practical. I believe that both are important for effectiveness - understanding the concepts, and implementing the practical learnings from the concepts. In many of the lectures, you will find both the conceptual and the practical mixed together. Think about the conceptual. Learn from the practical.

I recognize that you will also find a few duplications of stories, examples, and quotations. Keep in mind that these lectures were delivered over a period of more than two years. Refreshing the memory was useful in emphasizing a point for those attending the lectures. Hopefully, these duplications will serve as "memory enhancers" for you also.

Introduction to the Leadership Lectures

At AltaMed we included everyone from supervisor to CEO as members of the Leadership Development Institute. The principles and techniques of leadership and management are applicable at every level of an organization; thus, these lectures were prepared in such a way that they would be relevant to all supervisors, managers, and leaders. The techniques for leadership and management effectiveness can be utilized by the CEO. They can also be utilized by the front desk supervisor.

It should be noted that Castulo, our CEO, attended the sessions regularly. By doing so, he provided strong support for the Leadership Institute. Castulo was a leader, not only of his huge community health center network, but also as a supporter of the program. His participation did not go unnoticed by the staff of AltaMed.

I started out as a family practitioner doubling as the director of two storefront clinics in Indianapolis. More than three and a half decades in leadership roles later, with hundreds of missteps under my belt (and, hopefully, also many learnings), the idea of the Leadership Development Institute was born. Many of these hard-earned lessons are included in these lectures.

There are bits of practical wisdom sprinkled throughout these twelve lectures. Wisdom has to do with knowledge, discernment, and insight gained from both education and experience. My education regarding leadership and management was obtained through courses provided by the American College of Physician Executives. Completion of the courses resulted in certification as a physician executive (CPE). My experience comes from nearly 40 years in the trenches - fighting the battles, winning a few, and losing a good number of others.

Tell me, old timer,

> *"Where did you get your good judgment?"*
> *"From experience."*
> *"And where did you get your experience?"*
> *"From bad judgment."*

What you will read in these lectures emerged from the crucible of hard knocks. If you find concepts, ideas, or suggestions which are helpful to you and your organization, you are more than welcome to use them. That is this book's reason for being.

Chapter One

Leadership and the Rediscovery of Fire

> In order to talk about effective leadership, we must first understand what we are about and who we, as individuals, need to be. Beginning with thoughts about the meaning of life, this presentation peels away multiple layers in discussing the roles of love, respect, caring, compassion, and truly living our values in becoming effective leaders. It introduces the concepts of embracing change, proactivity, and the need to first change ourselves if we wish to change a situation.

The Touch of the Master's Hand

'Twas battered and scarred, and the auctioneer
Thought it scarcely worth his while
To waste his time on the old violin,
But he held it up with a smile.

"What am I bid, good friends?" he cried.
"Who'll start the bidding for me?
One dollar! Only one? And who'll make it two?
Two dollars, once. And three!

Three dollars, once. And three dollars, twice.
And going, and going," but no…
From the back of the room a grey-haired man
Came forward and picked up the bow.

And wiping the dust from the old violin,
And tightening every loose string,

He played a melody pure and sweet
As caroling angels sing.

The music ceased, and the auctioneer
With a voice that was quiet and low,
Said, "What am I bid for the old violin?"
As he held it up with the bow.

"One thousand dollars, and who'll make it two?
Two thousand dollars, and three!
Three thousand, once. And three thousand, twice.
And going, and going, and gone!" said he.

The people cheered, but some of them cried,
"We don't quite understand
What changed its worth?" Swift came the reply.
"Twas the touch of the Master's hand."

And many a man with life out of tune
And battered and scarred by life's din,
Is auctioned cheap to the thoughtless crowd
Much like this old violin.

A mess of pottage, a glass of wine.
A game, and he travels on.
He's going once, and going twice.
And going, and almost gone.

But the Master comes, and the thoughtless crowd
Never can quite understand
The worth of a soul, and the change that is wrought,
By the touch of the Master's hand.

Myra Brooks Welch, 1921[1]

The mission of AltaMed. Everyday, hundreds and hundreds of times, the people of AltaMed become the hands of the master. The touch of the master's hand happens every day, every hour, perhaps every minute, at AltaMed. For that, ultimately, is what we do.

Many of our patients, with life out of tune, and battered and scarred by life's din - much like the old violin - are going once, and going twice and going and almost gone.

And then they encounter the people of AltaMed. At AltaMed we recognize the worth of a soul. At AltaMed we recognize the change that can be wrought - by the touch of the physician's hand, and the social worker's hand, and the therapist's hand, and the dentist's hand, and the medical assistant and nurse's hands, and the transportation driver's hand, and the counselor's hand, in every case - the touch of the master's hand.

What I am about to share with you today will surprise you. For I am convinced that if we are going to talk about effective leadership, management, and supervision, we have to first back up, dig deep, peel away the layers and understand what we are about and who we, as individuals, need to be.

These are the two fundamental questions concerning effective leadership, management, and supervision. What are we about? (What are we really doing at AltaMed?) And who do we, as leaders, managers, and supervisors, need to be?

And what we are about is wiping the dust from the old violins, and tightening the loose strings, in order to play a melody as pure and sweet as a caroling angel sings. The master's hand. Our mission. Our reason for being. It is what we do everyday. What we are about, and what we do, at AltaMed.

The second question is who do we need to be? The remainder of this lecture will focus on the "who do we need to be" question.

Thinking about who we, as individuals, need to be brings me to a concept that will, at first, surprise you. Because today I want to talk with you about love. You are here for the first of a series on leadership, management, and supervision. I am going to begin talking about leadership by talking about love.

I am sure you are thinking, "Am I in the right room? I need to check my schedule. Is this the right meeting? Did I actually apply for the privilege of attending this lecture…on love…at AltaMed?"

As Julie Andrews sang in the Sound of Music: "Let's start at the very beginning. A very good place to start. When you read, you begin with a,b,c. When you sing, you begin with do-re-me."

When we talk about leadership and management at AltaMed, we must also go to the very beginning - the "do-re-me". The "do-re-me" is love. Love is the fundamental essence of our universe here at AltaMed. It is the focus that can make it all possible. As James Autry writes in <u>Love and Profit, the Art of Caring Leadership</u>, "Good management is largely a matter of love."[2]

There is a fundamental dynamic which must permeate each one of us, and which must permeate everything we do. And that dynamic is love.

Before this hour is over, you will hear other terms you did not expect to hear today—compassion, respect, values, proactivity. You will hear about the essential and fundamental traits of leaders and managers. (One term you are not going to hear, you will be pleased to know, is productivity. That's for later!)

Next month—transformational leadership. This month - love. If you want to be effective as a leader or as a manager or as a supervisor, you must know, and believe and live what you are about to hear.

What are we about at AltaMed? The touch of the master's hand.

And how do we do that? The time has come to talk about love.

Leadership and the Rediscovery of Fire

There is a phenomenal book out there. It is titled: <u>The Phenomenon of Man</u>.[3] It is written by French philosopher and theologian Pierre Teilhard de Chardin. It is basically about evolution and Christian thought. De Chardin proposes that the evolutionary developmental axis—from single cells to human kind—is the nervous system. He suggests that as the nervous system evolved over the millennia, and a brain began to develop which grew larger and more complex, there came a point in time when this brain, this nervous system, became so sophisticated that it suddenly was able to reflect inward—not just outward—introspection, not just reaction. This could have been the point where, as the Scriptures state, "God breathed into man the breath of life and man became a living soul."

Step with me, for just a brief moment, into the mind of Tielhard de Chardin.

Someday, after mastering the winds and the waves and the tides and gravity, we shall harness, for God, the energies of love. And then, for the second time in the history of the world, man will have discovered fire.

I have but one message for you today, and it is that harnessing the energies of love, the rediscovery of fire, must become the essence of the leadership, management, and supervision of AltaMed.

AltaMed started out a single little free clinic. A single cell, in the eyes of Teilhard de Chardin. And for more than forty years now, AltaMed has continued to grow. Just as Teilhard de Chardin's developmental axis is the nervous system, the developmental axis of AltaMed has been—and must continue to be—love and caring.

We all know the phenomenon of love. We all experience it in some way every day. But can you define it? What is your definition of love?

I have thought about love for a few years. Here is my definition. Two words. "Unconditional caring." Love is unconditional caring. Caring, no matter what. Unconditional.

And what is caring? Caring is when another person's existence matters to you.

When the existence of our patients, and the existence of our colleagues, matters to you - unconditionally - that is love. Leadership without love is only a shell. Management without love is hollow. If we can harness the energies of love, we will rediscover fire here at AltaMed.

AltaMed will survive if we focus on love and caring. Caring about AltaMed. Caring about our jobs. Caring about our patients. Caring about those we work with. Caring about our leaders. Caring about the quality of what we do. But if we become distracted - too much busy work to accomplish each day, and if we lose our focus - we may not survive. James Autry again: "Proper management involves caring for people, not manipulating them."[2]

An exceptional human being, Dr. Jack McConnell, lives on Hilton Head Island in South Carolina. He is a distinguished physician, scientist, and humanitarian. He is retired now. His career was with Johnson & Johnson. He was the Director of Advanced Technology. Johnson & Johnson told him to pursue whatever was of interest to him. He led the team that invented Tylenol. He played a key role in the development of MRI technology. He was active in unlocking the secrets of DNA. His son, by the way, plays keyboard for a band named Phish. You may have heard of it.

After he retired, he moved to Hilton Head. Michael Jordan has a home there. There are many wealthy gated communities on Hilton Head. Dr. McConnell looked around and discovered that there are also many medically indigent human beings living on the island. The support corps for the wealthy. And they had no accessible health care.

So he started "Volunteers in Medicine." He recruited the other retired physicians on Hilton Head to volunteer their time in their new clinic, funded by the other well-to-do residents. His Volunteers in Medicine concept—retired health care providers taking care of poor people for free—has now spread across this country. He even convinced Congress to provide free malpractice insurance for these volunteer providers by including them in the Federal Tort Claims Act program.

Dr. McConnell invited me out to Hilton Head to teach his staff about AmbuQual. (AmbuQual is the highly structured computer supported quality assessment program which we developed at HealthNet in Indianapolis.) I then invited Dr. McConnell to Indianapolis to teach my staff about compassion. He addressed our entire staff in the morning. Our staff members gave him a standing ovation.

During the day Dr. McConnell was asked if he could comment on the meaning of life. A simple question! What is the meaning of life? This man, who had already changed the world but was still working to make life better for the disadvantaged where he lived, thought for a moment. I have never forgotten his answer.

Life is a web of love. Our role is not to break that web, but rather to make it stronger.

The meaning of life: to strengthen the web of love.

This has to be what leadership, management, and supervision at AltaMed is all about—strengthening, living, and demonstrating the web of love for each other and for our patients.

Avedis Donabedian was recognized in the late 20th century as one of the true authorities on monitoring, measuring, and managing healthcare quality. This is what he said about the role of love: "Ultimately the secret of quality is love. You have to love your patient. You have to love your profession. You have to love your God. If you have love, you can then work backward to monitor and improve the system."[4]

I want to tell you another story—this one is more personal. When I was a freshman in high school, my brother and I shared a bedroom in the basement of our home in Winona Lake, Indiana. One stormy April night we awoke to find the entire wall of our bedroom on fire. The only exit from the bedroom was the door in that wall and out through the furnace room where the fire originated. All we could breathe was hot gaseous smoke. We went to the window of our basement bedroom, but could not get it open enough to get air – or to get out. The last thing I remember was thinking I had to get through that door and starting to run in that direction.

The fire chief of the Winona Lake volunteer fire department - wearing an air pack that the department had purchased just three days before, and tested that very morning - entered the burning room and found me unconscious, lying on the floor in front of the door. He found my brother lying under his bed.

One of my friends, visiting us in the hospital, left me a note that I think changed my life. He said, "God must have something important for you to do or the fire chief would not have been able to save you."

God must have something important for you to do. I suspect that is true for everyone here today. Or you would not be here. Something important to do. And so, because of what has happened to each one of us - our own personal stories - we appreciate life. We contribute to the web of love. And we get on with that important thing we have to do.

We are all shaped by our experiences. Each one of us has a story. AltaMed is more than one thousand people united around a common mission - the touch of the master's hand. Yet, we are more than one thousand people with uncommon experiences - forming the web of love - rediscovering fire.

We are people helping people.

Every day we have so many people trying so hard to strengthen that web of love, to achieve our vision of being Southern California's leading community-based provider of quality health care and human services.

How do we get there? May I suggest six fundamental concepts that will enable us to lead, manage, and supervise our organization toward world class. They all have to do with the web of love. Here is how I believe we should respond.

The first concept that will enable us to lead and manage our organization toward world class is to actually live our values. We hear a lot about our values around here. They are printed on our badges. We even have values awards. Several of you have been recipients. But have you internalized them? Do you know, and can you tell me, all six?

Why is it important to be thinking about AltaMed's values? Walt Disney's brother, Roy, was asked what was the secret to Disney's incredible success. He said, *"It is no secret. We've always tried to manage by our values because when you know what your values are, decision-making is easier."*[5]

Have you ever tried to prioritize our six values. Here is my prioritized version: 1) Integrity, honesty, and respect. 2) Employees are our most valuable asset. 3) Patients come first. 4) Encourage creativity. 5) Promote wellness. 6) Promote healthy communities. Each one with love and caring.

Make it a personal project to actually take the time to think very deeply about the meaning of each of AltaMed's values. What do they mean? What else could you do, that you don't already do, to truly live our values.

According to the Oxford dictionary a value is an abstract concept of what is right, worthwhile, and desirable. Are AltaMed's values right, worthwhile, and desirable? If so, live them like they are.

Here is something else. And this is really important. Can you articulate your own personal values? What three personal values are the most important to you? Examples of personal values could be kindness, patience, integrity, transparency, respect, fairness. Do you truly live your personal values every day?

As a leader, living your personal values is so important. You cannot effectively lead your people if cannot be sure what your personal values are. Your values determine why you do what you do. Why you decide what you decide. Your actions become grounded in fundamental personal values which drive you. They help you to focus on what is really important to you.

You need to think very deeply about what your personal values are and how to live them. Make a list. Prioritize these also to the top three or four. These become the values which drive you. Your vital few.

Finally, here is another reason that it is important to think about and live our values. Health care futurist, Leland Kaiser, has said that our vision as an organization is nothing more than our values projected into the future.[6] You will see what we will become.

The first concept: To become world class leaders, managers, and supervisors, we need to internalize and live our values, both AltaMed's values and our own personal values, everyday - with love. If we are not constantly focused on our values, we will never become world class leaders or managers and AltMed will never be world class in community health care.

The second concept that will enable us to lead and manage our organization toward world class is to <u>embrace change</u>. You will hear much about change in these sessions. Change is all around us. Change is the cause of many of our problems. Change is the solution to many of our problems.

AltaMed is going through a time of tumultuous change. And that is a good thing. The health care scene is changing fast. AltaMed's scene is changing fast. Healthcare futurist Leland Kaiser describes the pace of change in one word—breathtaking![6] AltaMed will be left behind if we don't get out in front of change. You personally will be left behind if you don't get out in front of change.

All of this change creates chaos. Chaos is everywhere. There is even a bit of chaos here at AltaMed! The greatest contributor to chaos is the one thing that is predictable in today's health care environment - change and its impact. It has been said that the only constant in today's world is exponentially increasing change.[7]

The second concept is to embrace change. So, what does this mean - to embrace change? Embrace means to clasp in your arms, hug, cherish, love. Embrace change. Webster's dictionary defines embrace as "to take up readily and gladly." Embrace change.

We must embrace change to enable AltaMed to survive in this chaotic environment. We must embrace change to enable each of us personally to survive in this chaotic environment. We must hug change, cherish change, and take it up readily and gladly.

Change produces so much stress. There is so much new stuff to deal with. However, what got us to where we are now will not get us to where we need to go in the future. We are going to have to change something.

Change is the cause. Change is also the solution. As I have said many times over the years, "If you want things to get better, you are probably going to have to change something."

I hope that you are bothered by all of this change. It has been said that the only people not bothered by change are the mindless. It is good if this change bothers you.

One thing about change, though. It can also be refreshing. Change embodies the hope of something better.

With love and caring, we need to lead our organization through unending change.

The second concept: As leaders, managers, and supervisors, in order to lead AltaMed toward world class, we must understand and embrace change.

The next two concepts that will enable us to lead and manage our organization toward world class are <u>respect and compassion</u>.

We must have respect and compassion for our patients. We must have respect and compassion for each other.

These two concepts, respect and compassion, become our own internal compass…our driving force. The way we are has much to do with our own degree of respect and compassion for others.

The way we are has much to do with our own degree of respect and compassion for others.

One of the things I have learned over the years is that everyone you meet is hurting in some way. If you just talk with them long enough, you will know why they are hurting. The person sitting to your right is hurting right now. And the person sitting to your left. For this reason alone, everyone deserves compassion and respect.

Our patients are hurting. Those you lead, manage, and supervise are hurting. We must lead with respect and compassion - with love and caring.

What is respect? *I would propose that respect is valuing each individual as worthwhile, lovable, and capable.*

Valuing each individual as worthwhile, lovable, and capable. The individual across from you—worthwhile, lovable, and capable. The individual next to you—worthwhile, lovable, and capable. The patient in front of you - worthwhile, lovable, and capable. Treat them that way. That is respect. As leaders and managers, we can lead the way - valuing each individual as worthwhile, lovable, and capable.

For our patients and for each other, we should:

Respect each other's differences. We must understand and accept our differences. In fact, we should value our differences.

Respect each other's humanness. We need to have a non-judgmental attitude. We all make mistakes. We all want the opportunity to try again in the morning.

Respect each other's deficiencies. We need to make a personal commitment to each other. We each have strengths. We each have weaknesses. All of us are unique.

Respect each other's ideas. Every idea is a good idea. It just might not be the right time and place. It could lead to an even better idea.

Respect each other's jobs. Every job is important. We don't have money in the budget for unimportant jobs.

Respect each other's opinions. Opinions are important. They reflect the thinking of a colleague. We can learn from other's opinions.

Respect each other's self-worth. Affirm each other and have a love for people.

We need to treat everyone - our colleagues, our staff, and our patients - as if they have a sign with large letters embroidered on their shirts: "I am worthwhile, lovable, and capable". That is what we all want to be, and that is what we all believe we are - worthwhile, lovable, and capable. We should respect each other and our patients as if they are wearing that sign.

Genuine respect is really not possible without love. Respect is what we owe. Love is what we give. Think of respect as being love in plain clothes. To be world class leaders, managers, and supervisors, we need to value everyone as worthwhile, lovable, and capable.

Then there is compassion. In spite of the fact that we would all say that in the health care world compassion is one of our strengths, compassion just may be a number one problem. How many horror stories do we hear in our centers that have at their roots a lack of compassion? We have written procedures that lack compassion. We have patients turned away every day because of a lack of compassion - they were late, or failed to bring the appropriate papers. We hear of rude staff members at the front desks or in the transportation vehicles.

Our patients exist in the poverty culture and we often don't recognize the uniqueness of their needs. Are we demonstrating a lack of compassion?

What is compassion? *Compassion is caring for others with sensitivity, understanding, and a deep feeling of concern - combined with a willingness to give aid.*

As leaders, managers, and supervisors, we can lead the way: caring for others with sensitivity, understanding, and a deep feeling of concern - combined with a willingness to give aid.

Jack McConnell, in describing his Volunteers in Medicine clinic, says that their motto is to take care of their "friends and neighbors" (they don't have "patients") with caring hands and loving hearts.[8] What a beautiful description of how we should take care of our patients, and take care of each other - with caring hands and loving hearts. This is the web of love.

Dr. McConnell talks of the mysterious chemistry which occurs when you give to someone in need. You are never again, according to Dr. McConnell, quite the same. When you give of yourself to someone in need, you are transformed. In the exam room, both the healer and the patient are never again quite the same. This mysterious chemical reaction comes from compassion. Compassion is not possible without love.

Compassion: caring for others with sensitivity, understanding, and a deep feeling of concern - combined with a willingness to give aid. Compassion with love and caring. Every day we offer caring hands and loving hearts.

The third and fourth concepts: As leaders, managers, and supervisors, in order to lead AltaMed toward world class, we must treat each other and treat our patients with respect and compassion.

Leadership and the Rediscovery of Fire

The fifth concept that will enable us to lead and manage our organization toward world class is <u>proactivity.</u>

Proactivity is a hugely important concept. It was described by Steven Covey in <u>Seven Habits of Highly Effective People.</u>[9] It is actually the first of the seven habits.

Essentially, proactivity means that as a human being you can choose how you will respond to a situation. Covey points out that in the interval between stimulus and response, humans have the ability to <u>choose</u>. Thus, our behavior becomes a function of our decisions, not a function of our conditions. Our feelings also become a function of our decisions, not our conditions.

Covey talks of the term "response...ability". Our ability to choose how we will respond.

According to Covey there are two types of people. Proactive people and reactive people. Highly proactive people do not blame circumstances, conditions, or conditioning for their behavior or morale. Their behavior or morale is a product of their own conscious choice, based upon values, rather than a product of their conditions. Proactive people can be effective leaders.

Reactive people, by decision or default, have chosen to empower conditions or conditioning to control them. Reactive people build their emotional lives around the behavior of others, empowering the weaknesses of other people to control them. Reactive people feel victimized and out of control. Reactive people are ineffective leaders.

It is not what happens to us, or our circumstances, but rather our responses that hurt us. Proactive or reactive. Which are you?

We hear a lot about morale in our community health centers. Mostly about how morale is low. Here is the bottom line on proactivity: Morale is not something that happens to you. Morale is how you choose to respond to situations.

If you choose to be unhappy, you will be unhappy. If you choose to be happy, you will be happy. You can choose to be miserable or you can choose to be strong. I have often said to my employees over the years, "I am responsible for the environment to which you are reacting, but I am not responsible for your reaction. You can choose what your morale will be. I assume no responsibility for your low morale."

Pain is inevitable. Misery is optional.

The fifth concept is to understand and accept ownership of our own responses. Proactivity is an essential component of love and caring. It will help us, as leaders, managers, and supervisors, to lead AltaMed toward world class.

Which brings me to the sixth and final concept: if we want to change the situation, we first have to <u>change ourselves</u>.

James Belasco in his book, <u>Flight of the Buffalo</u>, writes about how he discovered that as a leader, he had to change first, before he could get anyone else to change.[10]

We are talking about adaptability. The American Association for Physician Leadership includes adaptability as a leadership competency. It is defined as "flexibility, open to exploring new approaches and new priorities."[11]

If we want to change the situation, we first have to change ourselves. Adaptability.

If we want to have fun on the job, we have to become a fun person.

If we want a happy relationship, we have to become a happy person.

If we want to be trusted, we have to become trustworthy.

If we want the problems solved, we have to become a problem solver.

Eric Hoffer, dockside philosopher, made this profound observation:

Leadership and the Rediscovery of Fire

The remarkable thing is that we really love our neighbor only as much as we love ourselves. We do unto others as we do unto ourselves. We hate others when we hate ourselves. We are tolerant toward others when we tolerate ourselves. We forgive others when we forgive ourselves. It is not love of self, but hatred of self, which is at the root of the troubles that afflict our world.[12]

We respond by understanding that the way we treat others can be no different than the way we treat ourselves. And if we want to change something, we have to change ourselves.

As health care futurist, Leland Kaiser, has said, "The ability to transform an organization and our community is predicated upon the ability to transform ourselves."[6]

Being open and willing to change yourself to make a situation better, adaptability, is the fullest expression of love and caring.

The sixth concept: As leaders, managers, and supervisors, in order to lead AltaMed toward world class, we must be willing to change ourselves in order to change a situation.

Six concepts which we as leaders, managers and supervisors must internalize in order to be effective. Each of these six concepts grows out a fundamental foundation of love and caring.

1. Live our values.
2. Embrace change.
3. Respect each other and our patients.
4. Have compassion toward each other and toward our patients.
5. Be proactive.
6. If we want to change a situation, we first have to change ourselves.

The Leadership Lectures

Let me conclude with Victor Hugo. More than 150 years ago he wrote a powerful book entitled Les Miserables. You may have seen the musical. Or read the book. In the prologue to the book, he describes AltaMed's patients—100 years before AltaMed came into being!

This is what he said...

As long as there continues to exist, as a consequence of laws and customs, a social damnation artificially creating hells in the midst of civilization; as long as the three problems of the age—the degradation of man by the proletariat, the ruin of woman by hunger, and the atrophy of the child by the night—are not solved; as long as in certain regions social asphyxia shall be possible; as long as there shall be on the earth ignorance and wretchedness, books of the nature of this one cannot be useless.[13]

Or as we might say, "...then community health centers such as AltaMed cannot be useless."

At AltaMed, we must respond to the social damnation creating artificial hells in the midst of civilization.

At AltaMed we must respond to the degradation of man, the ruin of woman, and the atrophy of the child.

At AltaMed, we must respond to the social asphyxia, the ignorance, and the wretchedness which we see all around us.

And we must respond with caring, respect, compassion and love. In so doing, let us weave that web of love and let us make it stronger and stronger...for ourselves, for each other, for our communities, and for every single patient.

And now, this brings us back to Teilhard de Chardin's "harnessing the energies of love and for the second time in the history of the world, discovering fire."

When we at AltaMed can internalize and live these six concepts every day, when we at AltaMed can harness the energies of love, when we at AltaMed can become the master's hand for each and every patient, then we too will have rediscovered fire.

Chapter Two

The Five Fundamental Tasks of a Transformational Leader

> Here are five tasks that must become an everyday part of a leader's personal paradigm -- the way he or she does things. These tasks are critically important and together become the key to transformational leadership effectiveness.

Lester

Lester was given a magic wish
By the goblin who lives in the banyan tree,
And with his wish he wished for two more wishes -
So now, instead of just one wish, he very cleverly had three.

And with each of these three wishes
He simply wished for three more wishes,
Which gave him three old wishes, plus nine new.

And with each of these twelve wishes
He slyly wished for three more wishes,
Which gave him forty-six - or is it fifty-two?
Well anyway, with each wish
He wished for more wishes,
Until he had four million, seventeen thousand and thirty-four.

And then he spread his wishes on the ground
And clapped his hands and danced around
And skipped and sang, and then sat down
And wished for more.

And more…and more…they multiplied
While other people smiled and cried
And loved and reached and touched and felt.
Lester sat amid his wealth
Stacked mountain-high, like stacks of gold,
Sat and counted - and grew old.

And then one Thursday night they found him
Dead - with his wishes piled around him.
And they counted the lot and found that not
A single wish was missing.
All shiny and new - here take a few
And think of Lester as you do.

In a world of apples and kisses and shoes
Lester wasted his wishes on wishing.

Shel Silverstein[1]

"I wish that I could be more effective as a manager."

"I wish that I could spend less time putting out fires and more time building my program."

"I wish that I could manage change better."

"I wish that my people were as motivated as I am."

"I wish that I were more innovative."

"I wish that we all could see the same vision and move in the same direction together."

Wasting our wishes on wishing.

The Five Fundamental Tasks of a Transformational Leader

The point of the Leadership Development Institute is to get started turning our wishes into reality. Let's learn how to do this. Let's do what we need to do in order to become more effective.

Time now to move on to the topic for this session, the five fundamental tasks of a transformational leader.

It is easy to get caught up in the day-to-day management stuff. It is easy to spend your time firefighting. But my message for you today is that no matter how full your inbox, no matter how many people are standing at your door, no matter how many projects or reports or patients or problems or issues - you need to be continually thinking about these five fundamental tasks.

If you are to become a transformational leader, these five tasks need to become your own personal paradigm—the way you do things, the way you think, the way you approach things.

Here they are - the five fundamental tasks necessary for a transformational leader to move your organization from the way you did things in the past to where you need to be for the present and the future. 1) Define reality. 2) Articulate the vision. 3) Create alignment. 4) Become a servant. 5) Say "thank you."

Fundamental task #1 of a transformational leader: <u>Define reality.</u>

In order to be transformational in your leadership, in order to motivate your people to make the transition and inspire them to hang together while doing so, you must continuously define, discuss, and talk about reality - what is happening out there. The paradigm of the present.

Your staff must know and understand the context of your decisions. They must know what is happening. Staff react negatively to the decisions of their leaders because they do not know and do not understand the context.

I repeat: staff react negatively to the decisions of their leaders because they do not know and do not understand the context. Staff must know and understand what is happening. And to do that, you must be continually defining reality.

How do we define reality? Three thoughts:

The first thought: I believe that there is nothing more important for a transformational leader to do than periodic environmental scans—both external and internal. An environmental scan is really nothing more than describing what is out there right now and how it might be changing.

In the <u>external</u> environment: What is happening on the health care scene at the global level? What is happening at the national level? At the state level? At the local level? All of this is the external environment—external paradigms. What is happening in the external environment that may be changing the paradigms we are used to? Your staff needs to know and understand the context of your decisions.

In AltaMed's <u>internal</u> community health center environment: What is happening on the community health center scene at the national, state, and county levels? What is happening with the National Association of Community Health Centers? What is happening at the Bureau of Primary Health Care? What is happening at the level of our own Board? What is happening in the Executive Committee? What is happening in the internal environment that may be changing the paradigms we are used to? Your staff needs to know and understand the context of your decisions.

Define reality for your people. They must know the context.

And then as a leader, share with your staff how you see this playing out over the next twelve months. What will be the impact on our own little box? Our own paradigm?

The Five Fundamental Tasks of a Transformational Leader

The second thought: As part of defining reality, your staff must know and understand your Board's strategic response to this reality which you are defining. What is the Board doing to respond? What are the decisions being made by the Board? What are the strategies? How does the Board's strategic plan respond to current reality? The actions of the Board are another reality that you must continually define for your people. The same holds true for the Executive Committee. And if you do not know the answers to these questions about the Board and the Executive Committee, then you need to get yourself better connected.

The third thought: As a part of defining reality, your staff must know and understand why we are doing what we are doing. Your people need to know the <u>what</u>. They also need to understand the <u>why</u>. You need to focus on the why also.

Effective leaders manage meaning more than information. Your staff must know the why.

In order to be a transformational leader at any level, in order to move from one paradigm to the next, you must define reality – continually and never ceasing. Not once, but day after day. Week after week. Month after month.

Think about how and when we (and you) can do this. What forums can be used? Staff meetings. Perhaps you should have "reality roundtables". Maybe published updates for all staff. Perhaps invite the CEO and other senior leaders to your place, if you are in a satellite facility. Possibly other outside experts. Or just pay attention to what is happening all around you - and be your own "define reality" expert.

A big mistake in many organizations: the leaders do not spend enough time on fundamental task #1. And then they wonder why their staff is pushing back and is not interested in moving to the next paradigm. Staff must know and understand the context.

Fundamental task #1 of a transformational leader: Define reality…on a continuing basis.

Fundamental task #2 of a transformational leader: <u>Articulate the vision.</u>

The transformational leader has to describe where the organization wants to go—clearly and continuously. Once again this task, as with all of them, can relate to the entire organization, your division, your department, or your own particular area of responsibility. Articulate the vision.

As Charles Kettering, inventor, engineer, and holder of 186 patents, said, "My interest is in the future because I am going to spend the rest of my life there."[2]

I don't know who said this, but it could just as well have been Yogi Berra: "If you don't know where you are going, you might end up somewhere else."

We must have a vision and we must be continuously talking about it. You must be the #1 believer in the vision.

Here I am not referring exclusively to your organization's official vision. Rather, we are talking about your vision for what you can accomplish, or your division can accomplish, or your center can accomplish, or the nursing staff at your center can accomplish. <u>Your staff must continually hear you articulating your vision for your area of responsibility.</u>

Define reality. Then articulate the vision.

How do you do this? First, you must **create** your vision. Second, you must **sell** your vision. And third, you must **operationalize** your vision.

Create your vision: What is your vision for your own area of responsibility? It must be compatible with your current and future paradigms. It must be in the context of current reality. It must be consistent with your organization's official vision. Can you describe where you want your piece of the organization to be in two years? Five years? Ten years?

The Five Fundamental Tasks of a Transformational Leader

Your vision is not a description of where you are now (that is current reality). Rather, a vision is a description of where you want to be. A description of what you believe is possible - what you believe can be done.

You must create your vision.

Management expert Warren Bennis: "A vision articulates a view of a realistic, credible, attractive future for the organization; a condition that is better in some important ways than what now exists."[3] Create your vision.

Sell your vision: When you have created your vision, you must sell your vision. A vision does not mean anything to employees until they are hooked…until it means something to them.

How can you do this? Here are several suggestions: 1) Include your staff in the creation of your vision. 2) Relate current reality to the vision. 3) Be highly visible with your vision. 4) Make the vision a part of everyday conversation. Health Care consultant and lecturer Les Wallace would say you need to connect the dots.[4] Connect the everyday to your vision. Sell the vision.

Your vision statement should be on your walls. Could I walk through your areas and talk with your people and know what your vision is? Your vision statement will tell me where you are going. It will tell me that you are a transformational leader.

You must create your vision. You must sell your vision. And then, you must operationalize your vision.

Operationalize your vision: What does "operationalize" your vision mean? It means clearly communicating vision as it relates to each and every organizational effort, problem, opportunity, or decision.

Everything you do. Every decision you make. Every problem you address. Every opportunity you respond to—should be approached with your vision in mind. Will this move us closer to our vision?

An important part of who you are and what you do is your vision. Your vision should be on the walls of your organization. It should also be in the hearts and minds of your leaders, managers, and supervisors.

Here is a true story. One of my larger clinics in Indianapolis was really bogged down. As is often the case, processes were not working well. Staff were demoralized and tired. They were in a rut and actually were content to stay there. Nothing much was changing. In spite of my never-ending talk about our vision, the staff at this center did not seem to connect.

Eventually the staff seemed to collectively say, "Oh, we get it. Our leaders want us to change. They are describing what they want us to be. We are a long way away. We had better start chasing that vision." The staff made badges to wear, "Southeast Health Center: Out of the Stone Age." And they went to work. They caught the vision in their minds and hearts. The results were so astounding that the National Association of Community Health Centers published a monograph describing what they accomplished in their clinic.

Create the vision. Sell the vision. Operationalize the vision.

So task number two is to articulate the vision. Why is it so important? Because there is power in a vision. Why does a vision provide power? Because vision describes <u>possibility</u>. "This is something that we just might be able to do!" Healthcare futurist Lee Kaiser says, "The highest level of leadership is the creation of possibility."[5] Possibility provides power.

What is your vision for your area of responsibility? Your vision can inspire others to stretch…to look long range. Your vision describes possibility.

Your staff performs at one level because they have never thought about the possibility of performing at a higher level. The power of possibility.

The Five Fundamental Tasks of a Transformational Leader

You have to create your vision. You have to sell your vision. You have to operationalize your vision. And then you must lead utilizing the power of your vision.

What is your vision…for five years from now? Ten years from now? Vision is the creation of possibility. The highest level of leadership is the creation of possibility. A transformational leader articulates the vision.

The fundamental tasks of a transformational leader:

> Task #1: Define reality.
> Task #2: Articulate the vision.

Fundamental task #3 of a transformational leader: <u>Create alignment.</u>

We will never get to where we need to go if we are all going in different directions. We will never successfully make the transition to our next paradigm if we are all going in different directions. Creating alignment is a fundamental task of the transformational leader. It is a critical task in making the transition from the paradigm of the past to the paradigm of the future. Without alignment, we will surely fail.

Management guru Warren Bennis: "We must align human resources—creating a sense of shared objectives worthy of people's support… and even dedication. Great organizations inevitably develop around a shared vision."[6]

There are three steps to alignment. When thinking about how to create alignment as a transformational leader, we must think about these three steps—in this order. First, set the direction. Second, chart the course. And third, talk the walk.

> 1. Set the direction.
> 2. Chart the course.
> 3. Talk the walk.

Step one: Set the direction. What is the aim or direction of our organization? Our aim is expressed in our mission, vision, and values. Our direction.

Why do we exist? Our mission. People helping people.

What do we aspire to be? Our vision. Where we are going.

What do we believe in? Our values. What will guide us along the way. Our values become the core of stability in the vortex of change.

Collins and Poras in <u>Built to Last: Successful Habits of Visionary Companies</u> observe, "A visionary company almost religiously preserves its core ideology—changing it seldom, if ever."[7] Set the direction.

Your direction is set by your Board. It is described in your mission, your vision, and your values. Your rock solid foundation. As leaders, managers, and supervisors, you must understand, buy into, and constantly remind your people of your direction.

Step one in creating alignment: Set the direction.

Step two: Chart the course. We know our aim. We know our vision. Now as transformational leaders committed to alignment, we have to show our people how to get to that vision. We must chart the course.

In order to chart the course, we must organize around specific strategies, specific priorities and specific objectives. At every level, our people must be constantly reminded of our aim, and they must know the course—our objectives. And our objectives must be aligned if we expect our people to be aligned.

Step one in creating alignment: Set the direction. Step two: Chart the course.

Step three: Talk the walk. Alignment is a communications problem, not a design problem. You must be constantly talking with your people. Talk the walk. Often one-on-one encounters. You must help each of your people to understand reality, to share the vision, to internalize your aim, and to buy into the course that we have charted. Your goal is for

The Five Fundamental Tasks of a Transformational Leader

each of your people to be pointed in the same direction. As John Ketter wrote in the Harvard Business Review, "We don't want to organize people. Rather, we want to align people."[8]

Be alert to which of your people are out of alignment. Be alert to people straying off course. And then, talk the walk.

To create alignment: 1) Set the direction. This is done for you by the Board. Communicate that direction to your people. 2) Chart the course. Often you help to create the course. Make it happen. And 3) Talk the walk. Everyday.

Leadership is about alignment. Alignment is everything.

Let me repeat that: *Leadership is about alignment. Alignment is everything.*

Fundamental task number three: Create alignment.

The fundamental tasks of a transformational leader:

> Task #1: Define reality.
> Task #2: Articulate the vision.
> Task #3: Create alignment.

Fundamental task #4 of a transformational leader: Become a servant.

Have you heard the term "servant leadership"? There are books written about servant leadership. How can you be a servant and a leader at the same time? How does this make you transformational?

By becoming a servant leader, you are recognizing the tremendous and mostly untapped potential of your people. Let me repeat: By becoming a servant leader, you recognize the tremendous and mostly untapped potential of your people

If you can just help them to achieve their potential, think how your organization will be transformed. If you can just get out of their way and give them the support they need, think of what they might accomplish. You need to be a supportive leader. You need to be a servant leader.

There are four steps to becoming a servant leader: 1) Provide a supportive environment. 2) Walk the talk (not talk the walk, as above). 3) Empower your people. 4) Nurture bottom up change.

Step one: Provide a supportive environment. The servant leader is a supportive leader. The question constantly on the servant leader's tongue is, "How can I make things better for you?" The environment which you create for your people needs to be a supportive environment. Your people need to be confident in your support. Your people need to be confident that they can try new things, take risks, even make mistakes, and you will be supportive. Effective leaders know that wisdom is the art of knowing what to overlook.

That was important. Let me say it again. When it comes to your people and what they do and don't do, *"Wisdom in leadership is the art of knowing what to overlook."* Are you supportive, no matter what?

Much of what we talked about in our first session had to do with becoming a supportive leader. Love, compassion, respect, helping our people to achieve their potential, proactivity. All create a supportive environment.

We at AltaMed have created the AltaMed support chart. It has been approved by the Executive Committee and the Board.

The AltaMed support chart is all about the supportive environment. It is all about becoming a servant leader. It flips the organization over. It recognizes what AltaMed is all about. The Board is at the bottom of this chart. Then the CEO and the Vice Presidents - supporting the rest of the organization. Then the managers and the supervisors and the support services. And finally, at the top, the people who come face to face with our patients. The supportive environment.

Kouzes and Posner in their book, <u>The Leadership Challenge</u>, say, "Leadership is service. Leaders become servant leaders - not self-serving, but other serving. The relationship of leaders and constituents has been turned upside down. Or rather, it has been righted."[9]

Step one in becoming a servant leader: Provide a supportive environment.

Step two: Walk the talk. To create alignment, we talk the walk. To be a servant leader, we walk the talk

What does this mean…to walk the talk? It means exactly that. We talk about living our values. If you are a servant leader, you actually do live the values. We talk about embracing change. You very visibly embrace change. We talk about demonstrating respect and compassion. You do that - every day and in every way. We talk about being proactive. You choose positive responses consistently. We talk about needing to change yourself on occasion; you actually do when it is necessary. You walk the talk. A servant leader.

When you walk the talk, you are present on the battlefield. You spend your time outside of your office. Possibly one of the single most dramatic things you could do at your organization to increase the effectiveness of your managers would be to eliminate their offices. You can't sit in your office if you do not have one. (You understand that I said this to get your attention. But, hopefully, you get the point!) To be a servant leader you need to be out there on the battlefield every day.

Every action needs to visibly demonstrate a true commitment. You must set the example. When was the last time you were out on the front sidewalk picking up the cigarette butts in front of your facility to create a more pleasing entryway for your patients? When was the last time you were in cleaning up the bathroom for your patients? You must believe in our core values so strongly that you would not even think twice about doing this. You set the example. You go first. You walk the talk. You become a servant.

Another way to walk the talk is to "walk in the moccasins". Have you done that? Spend some time doing the job of one of your people. You cannot fully appreciate what they do until you have walked in their moccasins. I did that in Indianapolis. Over a period of several years actually. Every single job in my organization. At least a half a day for each one. I learned a ton. Your people will love it. Seeing you sitting there scratching your head. They will respect you more. You will respect them more. You can walk the talk by walking in the moccasins.

Step two in becoming a servant leader: Walk the talk. Model being a servant.

Step three: Empower your staff. Empowerment is a difficult, confusing, yet important and powerful concept.

As a servant leader committed to providing a supportive environment, you are constantly asking your people, "How can I make things better for you?"

As a servant leader committed to empowering your staff, you are constantly asking your people, "How can I help you make things better?" Did you pick up on the difference? Not how can I make things better for you, but rather how can I help you make things better? Empowerment.

Why is it important to empower your staff? There is exponential potential in empowerment. Think of the combined IQ of an empowered organization. At AltaMed we have a seven member Executive Committee. Seven members. If the average IQ is 110 (and some staff members would say that is a high estimate), then the decision-making empowerment quotient at AltaMed is 770 IQ volts. If we empowered all of our 800 or so AltaMed people to participate in the decisions of AltaMed, we might multiply the 110 average IQ times 800. The decision-making empowerment quotient at AltaMed then becomes 88,000 IQ volts - 770 vs. 88,000. The exponential potential of empowerment.

Being a servant leader means recognizing the potential of your people and creating opportunities for them to participate in transforming your organization - choosing and then moving toward the paradigm of the future.

The servant leader creates a culture of empowerment. What happens then?

The Five Fundamental Tasks of a Transformational Leader

First: A culture of empowerment provides people with the sense that they are at the center of things. They are involved. They are invested. Empowerment.

Second: A culture of empowerment unleashes the talent of other people. Leadership is not about being talented yourself. It is about freeing the talents of others. Empowerment.

Third: A culture of empowerment liberates the leader in everyone. Kouzes and Posner again: "If everyone is a leader (through empowerment), then everyone is responsible for guiding the organization toward its future."[9] <u>Put everyone in charge of something</u>. Empowerment.

And what do you, the servant leader, do? You get out of the way. Your empowered people will move your part of the organization forward. And you are not afraid to let them do this because you have already created alignment. Your empowered staff will move you in the direction you need to go.

Step three in becoming a servant leader: Empower your staff.

Step four: Nurture "bottom-up" change. Changing from the top down works when things are stable. It is more difficult when between paradigms - the unstable transition phase. Here people are resisting change, pushing back.

As a servant leader, encourage your people to make things better. To change whatever needs to be changed. Watch for change occurring at the bottom, nurture it when you see it beginning to happen, and go with it whenever it occurs. Don' fret about whether or not it is a good idea. It probably is. And it is likely to be better than what you might have come up with. If it isn't a good idea, that will become clear soon enough.

It has to do with creating alignment, empowering your staff and then getting out of the way. Support the change. Be a servant. Celebrate both the triumphs and failures. Your people can "try again in the morning."

Remember this: people don't mind changing. They just mind being changed. If you see people ready to change something, nurture that. Let them do the changing.

Step four in becoming a servant leader: Nurture "bottom-up" change.

And so, fundamental task #4 is to become a servant. The four steps: 1) provide a supportive environment, 2) walk the talk, 3) empower your staff, and 4) nurture "bottom-up" change.

The CEO of a major corporation has on his business card, not his title, but rather "Chief Servant."

The fundamental tasks of a transformational leader:

>   Task #1: Define reality.
>   Task #2: Articulate the vision.
>   Task #3: Create alignment.
>   Task #4: Become a servant.

Fundamental task #5 of a transformational leader: Say "Thank you."

Finally, we get to a fundamental task that initially sounds simple and easy to do. On the contrary, it is not simple at all. In fact, it may be the most profound and important of all five tasks. You need to be profuse but genuine in your thank you's. Your thank you's should be continuous and highly visible.

The Gallup employee satisfaction survey identifies the 12 most significant employee satisfiers in successful companies. Significantly, having the employee's supervisor thank them for their good work during the past 10 days made the list. Being thanked on a regular basis is listed as one of the major satisfiers for employees.

The Five Fundamental Tasks of a Transformational Leader

The two most important two-word phrases that you should use without hesitation in order to be an effective leader: "My fault'" and "Thank you." "Thank you" is one of the five fundamental tasks of an effective leader. There are very few things at work that are more gratifying than a genuine "thank you."

As leaders, managers, and supervisors, at the end of the day, go find someone who has helped you - front desk, medical records, medical assistant, nurse, providers, lab, x-ray, secretaries, or even the clinic manager - and thank them for helping on that particular day. Make it a daily habit. Thanking someone who has helped you may be the most important thing you do all day.

Most organizations have formal mechanisms for expressing appreciation. Use them. At AltaMed, we have formal recognition cards. Supervisors or others can formally recognize good performance. A copy goes to the employee's personnel file. We fill out about 250 cards per year. That sounds like a lot, but averages out to be about 1/3 of a card per employee per year. AltaMed employees can anticipate getting formal recognition only once every three years! Use the system.

Staff appreciation events and other celebrations are good. We should continue. But the personal is best.

As Otto Van Ish said, "I have yet to be bored by someone paying me a compliment."[10]

The last, and likely the most important, of the five fundamental tasks is to say "Thank you." Every day. Don't go home until you have said "Thank you" to at least one person.

No matter whether you are a leader, a manager, or a supervisor, the fundamental tasks of a transformational leader are the five fundamental tasks for you.

> Task #1: Define reality.
> Task #2: Articulate the vision.
> Task #3: Create alignment.

Task #4: Be a servant.
Task #5: Say "Thank you".

Think of these every day. You need each one in order to be effective. Put these five on your mirror at home so that you see them first thing in the morning. Review them in your mind as you are driving to work. Make them a part of the way you think. The way you do things.

Turning your wishes into reality. This is how you do it.

And think of Lester and his wasted wishes as you do.

Chapter Three

Building the Mental Model for Leadership

> Four critical components must be considered when crafting the mental model for becoming a transformational leader. This lecture defines these components and discusses them in detail. The mental model described is an important prerequisite in developing a personal leadership philosophy.

I Am Falling Off a Mountain

I am falling off a mountain,
I am plummeting through space,
You can see this does not please me
By the frown upon my face.

The ground keeps getting closer,
It's a simple fact to tell,
That I have a slight dilemma,
That my day's not going well.

My velocity's increasing,
I am dropping like a stone,
I could do with some assistance,
Is there someone I could phone?

Though I'm not afraid of falling,
I am prompted to relate,
That the landing has me worried,
And I don't have long to wait.

The Leadership Lectures

My options are decreasing,
There's just one thing left to try—
In the next eleven seconds,
I have got to learn to fly.

Jack Prelutsky[1]

Learning to fly. In the beginning, it was playing the violin. The touch of the master's hand. Then it was all about Lester, his magic wishes, and five fundamental tasks. Today, it is learning to fly.

They're all the same. They are about our effectiveness as leaders, managers, and supervisors. Effectiveness has to do with knowing <u>how</u>. And that is why we are here. Violin virtuosity or flying do not come naturally. You have to work at it. Day after day. Month after month. Year after year. There is no magic wish. You have to know how.

You have to work at leadership also. Day after day. Month after month. Year after year. You have to know how. There are very few natural born leaders. You have to study leadership. You have to understand leadership. You have to practice leadership. You have to fail at leadership. And as a leader, when you fail, you try again in the morning.

We all seem to fall off a lot of mountains. We need to learn to fly.

This month: building the foundation for a transformational leadership model. Your mental model of leadership. How to think about leadership. There are four infrastructure components which are important to understand as you begin to sort out this leadership thing.

You are going to hear much in these sessions about becoming a transformational leader. You are also going to hear much about the notion that whether your title is leader, manager, or supervisor, you still need to be a leader. You need to be a transformational leader.

Fundamental component number one for your leadership mental model: You must understand that a transformational leader leads from one paradigm to the next.

Building the Mental Model for Leadership

We recently talked about the five fundamental tasks of a transformational leader. So let's now look at what we mean by "transformational leader." The first of the four components. Here the bottom line is that a transformational leader is one who is capable of *leading the organization from one paradigm to the next.*

Do you recall what a paradigm is? "Paradigm" is just a convenient word for the way we think. The way we do things. The way we approach things. Our health care model.

Here is how the American Heritage dictionary defines the word paradigm: *"A set of assumptions, concepts, values, and practices that constitutes a way of viewing reality for the community that shares them."*

Our current assumptions, concepts, values, and practices constitute our paradigm of the present.

A paradigm of the past is the way we used to do things. If it is a paradigm of the past, we don't do things that way anymore. Our previous health care model. Describe the way the medical clinics operated ten years ago. That was the paradigm of the past.

A paradigm of the future is the way we will be doing things - two years from now, five years from now, ten years from now. Leaders should visualize the way our clinics could be operating 5-10 years from now. You would be visualizing a paradigm of the future.

Paradigms change. The way we do things, the way we think about things, change. Sometimes they just change on their own over time—they evolve. Other times they change because we make the decision that they need to change - or must change. And we set about changing the paradigm.

Don't be intimidated by the word. It is simply a convenient way to describe the sum total of our assumptions, concepts, values, and practices.

The Leadership Lectures

In the first lecture, we talked about the "breathtaking" pace of change in health care. We talked about how things are changing so fast that "What got us to where we are now will not get us to where we need to be in the future." [2] We need a new paradigm.

We need to think differently. We need to do things differently, approach things differently. We need a new model. The paradigm of the past will not work in the future. Our leaders need to be able to lead us from the paradigm of the past to the paradigm of the future.

Transformational leaders lead to the next paradigm.

But here is a critical concept: Managers and supervisors also play a key role in moving the organization from one paradigm to the next. The leaders cannot do it by themselves.

It is the leader's primary responsibility to position the organization correctly for the future. Transformational leadership. Managers and supervisors also have to be transformational. Ready, willing, and able to change "on a dime" whenever it is necessary.

For a transformational leader to be successful, three points are obvious.

1) *The first obvious point is that the transformational leader must choose the correct next paradigm.* It is clear to the transformational leader that something has to change. The organization needs a new paradigm in order to thrive in the future. But what should that paradigm be?

Hitler planned to move Germany to a new paradigm. He was a transformational leader. He chose a bad paradigm and ultimately was unable to move his country successfully from one paradigm to another.

In the 80s, IBM was a mainframe computer company. IBM was also struggling because, as urban commentator David Stein pointed out, the "past was gone, and the present was full of confusion." [3] The leaders of IBM made the decision that the company needed to change paradigms, and needed to do it quickly. IBM decided to make laptops, the Think Pad was born, and the rest, as they say, is history. A very successful move from the paradigm of the past to an effective paradigm for the future.

Here is the question we cannot ignore. If the transformational leader must choose the correct next paradigm, how can we be sure we are choosing the correct paradigm?

The answer is a simple one: We can't be sure. At the Board and CEO level, we may not know for 5-10 years if we have chosen the correct next paradigm. I believe we are between paradigms right now here at AltaMed. We are moving toward the paradigm of our future. Is it the correct next paradigm? We hope so. But we may not know for some time.

Thus, it becomes a matter of making a very thoughtful decision. As leaders, part of our job description (and compensation) is to think. And think we must. We must understand the past. We must understand our paradigms of the past. The way we used to do things. We must be fully aware of what is happening in the present. We must analyze the present carefully. We must pick it apart, piece by piece. We must visualize the future. Visualize where AltaMed's best fit for the future might be - or the best fit for your own particular area of responsibility. And when you have thought about this as much as you can possibly think, then choose the next paradigm.

Once you choose the next paradigm, you cross your fingers and hope; but you also work as hard as you possibly can to make it a success. You stay alert and are quick to make midcourse corrections when necessary.

The transformational leader must choose the correct next paradigm.

2) *The second obvious point is that the leader must motivate the organization to make the paradigm leap along with her or him.* We all prefer things the way we are used to. Changing to a new paradigm is scary. Every organization will resist change. A transformational leader is able to motivate the

organization to take a deep breath and make the big leap, believing that the new paradigm, chosen by its leaders, is the right thing to do and, in fact, is the only thing to do.

The transformational leader must motivate the organization to move to the next paradigm.

3) *The third obvious point is that a transformational leader must inspire the organization to hold together while in the very dangerous transition phase between paradigms.* Between paradigms is a dangerous and volatile place to be. We have left the security of doing things the way we did them in the past. We have not yet settled into the new way to respond to the future. People get uncomfortable. Things can blow up. Life in the organization is not stable. People get emotional and tense. Actions or comments are easily misinterpreted. Flare-ups occur. Little things become big things.

The transformational leader must inspire the organization to hold together between paradigms.

All of us - leaders, managers, and supervisors - must be alert to the symptoms of instability while we are between paradigms. Watch out for the little things. Stay focused on what we have to do. And take care of each other. If we are unsuccessful in making the transition between paradigms, it will be because we did not take care of each other.

Component number one: Transformational leaders lead to the next paradigm. We all - leaders, managers and supervisors - play a key role in the transformation. Our leaders cannot do it alone. Managers and supervisors make it happen.

Fundamental Component number two for your leadership mental model: You must understand the present in the context of the past and then anticipate the future in the context of the present.

Building the Mental Model for Leadership

Each one of us must open our eyes to what is happening in health care all around us. And we need to understand what is happening now - the present - from the perspective of the past. And we need to look at what could be happening in the future from the perspective of the present. This is a huge leadership challenge. Understanding what is happening.

Let me say that again: Understanding what is happening is a huge leadership challenge.

As David Stein said, *"The past is gone. The present is full of confusion. And the future scares the heck out of me."* [3]

Let us first comment on the <u>past</u>. Some of you may be old enough to remember the past. Often referred to as the good old days. (Although they may not have seemed so "good old" at the time!) I actually spent more than 30 years leading and managing in the past.

From today's perspective, the past seems relatively simple. And relatively predictable. As the leader of a community health center network, I pretty much knew for sure that if we kept on doing what we were doing, we would still be around the next year…and the year after that.

Managed care had not been invented yet. There were no health care plans to tell us what to do. Or to do site visits or inspections. There was no such thing as HIPAA. The Joint Commission ambulatory standards manual was about 25 pages long. OSHA was a non-factor. No safety officers. No compliance officers. No privacy officers. No practice management computer systems. No electronic medical records. We just took care of our patients. In fact, when we first started our little store front clinics in Indianapolis, we had a jar on the receptionists desk for the patients to drop in their quarter. That was their fee for the visit. No encounter forms. We started our receptionists at $1.78 per hour and our MA's at $1.89 per hour.

We just took care of our patients. With loving hands and caring hearts. And we did a pretty good job.

The past: control, order, predictability. Leadership was really pretty easy back then. The problem is, as pointed out by David Stein, the past is gone. And it is <u>really</u> gone.

And now for the <u>present</u>. The present is full of confusion. Global change, uncertainty, complexity and chaos. The present is not like the past at all.

47% of the 1980 Fortune 500 companies no longer exist in the present. Half. Half of the 1980 Fortune 500 companies encountered the present and did not survive.

Warren Bennis, management guru, asks: *"How do you change relatively successful organizations, which, if they continue to act today the way they acted even five years ago, will undo themselves in the future?"* [4]

Half of the 1980 Fortune 500 companies continued to act in the way that made them successful - and in so doing "undid" themselves.

What got us to where we are now, will not get us to where we need to be in the future.

At AltaMed, we have run headfirst into the present. It is not like the past. Complexity, chaos, uncertainty. In your gut you know that if we continue to do things the way we did them in the past, our organization will not survive.

David Stein: *The present is full of confusion.* As leaders, managers and supervisors, we must guide our staff and our programs through the confusion and chaos of the present. To do that, we must open our eyes to what is happening all around us, and respond appropriately. We have to become transformational in our leadership.

And so, what about the <u>future</u>? Unpredictible.

Modern day philosopher, the late Yogi Berra: *"The future ain't what it used to be."*

Or as former Kansas City Royals pitcher Dan Quisenberry observed: *"I have seen the future, and it is like the present, only longer."* Not a real comforting thought, actually.

Who has a clear idea of what health care will look like five years from now? Of what AltaMed will look like five years from now? The only predictable thing right now is unpredictability.

David Stein: *The future scares the heck out of me.* There is only one way to avoid the fate of half of the Fortune 500 companies. We have to become transformational in our leadership.

The past is gone. The present is full of confusion. And the future scares the heck out of me.

The second leadership mental model component that we all must understand: We must open our eyes to what is happening in health care and at AltaMed. We must accept that the past is gone. We must recognize that the present is chaos and confusion. And we must admit that the future is unpredictable.

If we fail to do this, if we continue on our present course, we will fail as leaders, managers, and supervisors. Pay attention. Be ready. Be innovative. Be flexible. Be creative. Be anxious to change.

Let me say that even though unpredictable, there is definitely hope for our future. If we pay attention. If we choose the correct next paradigm, AltaMed will have a great future. Our vision will become reality.

Fundamental leadership component number two useful in crafting your mental model of leadership: Understanding the past, the present, and the future.

Fundamental component number three for your leadership mental model: You must understand leadership in the context of management and management in the context of leadership.

The Leadership Lectures

John P. Kotter is the Konosuki Matsushita Professor of Leadership at Harvard Business School and a frequent speaker at top management meetings around the world. He is the author of six bestselling books on leadership. He makes the point: *Strong leadership needs strong management.*[5] The reverse, no doubt, is also true. Strong management needs strong leadership.

To be a good leader and to be a good manager, you must understand the difference.

The philosophy of our Leadership Development Institute is that leadership and management are two ends of a continuum. Everyone in this room who is a leader or manager or supervisor is located at some point on this continuum. If you are basically a leader, you still have management responsibilities. If you are basically a manager, you still have leadership responsibilities.

We need to start, though, with the fundamental difference between leadership and management.

Think about this scenario: We want to get from one end of the jungle to the other. <u>Leader</u> - gets out the topographical map and lays out the best route for a road. <u>Manager</u> - builds the road.

Another scenario: Building a new million-dollar house. The architect has the vision and designs the house. The architect is the leader. The contractor has the skills and builds the house. The contractor makes it happen. The contractor is the manager.

Think about these complementary functions:

Leadership: *about coping with change.*
Management: *about coping with complexity.* (No one ever said that management is easy!)

Leadership: *developing a vision and strategies to achieve the vision.*
Management: *planning, budgeting, and allocating resources.*

Building the Mental Model for Leadership

Leadership: *leading between paradigms.*
Management: *managing within paradigms.*

Leadership: *motivating and inspiring.*
Management: *controlling and problem solving.*

Leadership: *strategic thinking.*
Management: *planning.*

Leadership: *determining the right thing to do.*
Management: *determining how to do things right.*

Leadership: *satisfying basic human needs for achievement, a sense of belonging, recognition, self-esteem.*
Management: *"helping normal people who behave in normal ways to complete routine jobs successfully day after day."*[6]

Leadership: *getting people to want to do what needs to be done.*
Management: *getting people to do what needs to be done.*

Leadership: *pull.*
Management: *push.*

We need both—leaders and managers. A vision will never become a reality if the architect does not have a contractor - if the leader does not have a manager. Leaders decide what needs to happen. Managers make it happen. I cannot emphasize enough how important strong management is. Strong leadership needs strong management.

Where are you on the continuum? A frequent mistake in many organizations is that the leaders become too involved in management - in many cases, a science at which they are not very good. The flip side is also true - managers fancy themselves leaders. Both have significant negative consequences. You end up with people who are not good at management trying to manage. And people who are not cut out to be leaders, trying to lead.

This does not mean that if you are a leader you do not need management skills, or if you are a manager, you do not need leadership abilities. The fact of the matter is that none of us is totally at one end or the other of the spectrum. An architect who does not understand how to build a house will not be an effective architect, nor will a contractor who does not understand the principles of architectural design be an effective contractor. That is why we think it important for all of us in these training sessions to be exposed both to leadership principles and to management techniques.

Fundamental component number three, useful in crafting your leadership mental model: understanding the relationship between leadership and management.

Fundamental component number four for your leadership mental model: You must understand about nesting paradigms.

In order to understand component number four, we need to go back to the concept of paradigms. The way we think. The way we do things. The way we approach things. Our health care model.

Here is a critically important concept: *There are paradigms at all levels.* There are paradigms within paradigms.

You may have seen nesting dolls or nesting eggs - progressively smaller and smaller ones inside the larger ones. For this discussion, nesting boxes would make an even better example than nesting dolls or eggs.

We have talked about AltaMed's paradigm. Here is the point of component number four: The way we think and approach things at the highest levels of AltaMed - our global AltaMed paradigm—is in response to an even larger paradigm, the health care environment for the underserved in Los Angeles County - Plans, County Clinics, County Hospital, MediCal patients, etc. Our way of doing things (our paradigm) takes place within the LA paradigm. And the two have to be aligned. In fact, the larger paradigm will devour the smaller paradigm if they are not compatible. The Pac Man phenomenon.

Building the Mental Model for Leadership

The larger paradigm (the County's) is changing fast, because it itself is a smaller paradigm - in the State of California, and in the nation. And because the national, state, and county paradigms are changing, AltaMed's paradigm has to change, also. Or else we are history. Our leaders have to choose the correct next paradigm for AltaMed.

Here is where I am going with this. Nested within the AltaMed paradigm (the way we think, the way we do things at AltaMed) are smaller and smaller paradigms. Smaller, but no less important. Within the AltaMed paradigm are possibly three smaller paradigms - of the medical division, of the long term care division and of the support services in the broadest sense. Each has its way of doing things, approaching things, thinking about things - their model, their paradigm.

Just as at the higher level, these paradigms have to be compatible with AltaMed's paradigm or they will not survive - at least their leaders will not survive. The Vice Presidents at this level also have to choose the correct next paradigm, motivate their people to move to that paradigm, and inspire everyone to hold together during the transition.

Take this a step further. Within the Medical Division, for example, are a number of even smaller paradigms - those of the clinics. All similar in the way they think, but with their own uniqueness's. The co-leaders of the clinics - administrative managers and site lead clinicians - must also choose the correct next paradigm, motivate, and inspire. And the paradigm they choose must be compatible with the larger paradigms.

Finally, within the individual medical clinic paradigms are even smaller, but equally as important, paradigms. An example might be the front desk paradigm - the way they do things, approach things; their model. Here it is the front desk supervisor who becomes transformational - leading his or her group from one paradigm to the next. Compatible with the larger paradigms? Absolutely. If the larger paradigms change, the front desk staff must change their paradigm also. Or else they will be out of synch.

And so, whether you are the Chairman of the Board, or CEO, or a vice president, or a manager or a site lead clinician, or a supervisor - you need to be a transformational leader. You are responsible for leading your organization (or your part of the organization) from one paradigm to the next.

Every leader at every level has to be alert to what is happening. Every leader at every level must study and understand the larger paradigms. Pay attention. And then, when things are changing, you - the transformational leader - must choose the correct next paradigm—whether it is for your front desk unit, your clinic, your division, or AltaMed as an organization. And then you must motivate your people to move to that paradigm and inspire them to hang together during the transition.

One final thought: You have your own personal paradigm. The way you are. The way you think, do things, approach things. Your values. Your leadership philosophy. Your life model. Is your personal paradigm consistent with the AltaMed paradigm within which you work? Your job will be the most fulfilling if your personal paradigm is in synch with your organization's paradigm.

A transformational leader leads to the next paradigm. All of us - leaders, managers, and supervisors - have an important role to play in this transformation.

The concept of the nesting paradigms.

The past is gone. We must abandon the paradigm of the past. The present is full of confusion. In the midst of this confusion we must make thoughtful and rational decisions about how to position AltaMed (or the area for which you are responsible) for the future. And though the future is unpredictable, we can't wait. We must transform our organization in order for AltaMed to be compatible with the larger paradigms of the future.

Transformational leaders. Everyone in this room.

Fundamental component number four: The nesting paradigms.

Building the Mental Model for Leadership

These four components become an integral part of your mental model of leadership:

1. The transformational leader leads between paradigms.
2. Understanding that the past is gone, the present is full of confusion, and the future is unpredictable.
3. The role of leadership vs. that of management.
4. The concept of the nesting paradigms.

We started off today's session by falling off a mountain and deciding that we needed to learn to fly. And soon.

You can't fly if you don't have wings. Just as you can't play the violin without strings. What we are about here in our Leadership Development Institute is developing the wings and tightening the strings…so that each one of us can achieve our potential and become maximally effective as leaders, managers, and supervisors.

The web of love is important. Those six concepts relating to the rediscovery of fire are important. The five fundamental tasks of a transformational leader are important. These four leadership mental model components are important.

They all can help you fly.

Chapter Four

Crafting Your Personal Leadership Philosophy

> This presentation covers the importance of thinking through, writing out, and then living one's personal leadership philosophy. A clearly articulated leadership philosophy underpins leadership effectiveness. .

'Tis the Set of the Sail

One ship sails east and another sails west,
With the selfsame winds that blow;
'Tis the set of the sails and not the gales
That tells them where to go.

Like the winds of the sea are the winds of time,
As we journey along through life;
'Tis the set of the soul that determines the goal,
And not the calm or the strife.

Ella Wheeler Wilcox, 1916[1]

Today, we will begin discussing the development of your personal leadership philosophy. Your personal leadership philosophy is about the set of your sails. If your sails are set correctly, your personal leadership philosophy - not the gales you encounter every day - will tell you where to go. Everyone in this room - no matter what your position - should have a personal leadership philosophy. Do you know what yours is?

Crafting Your Personal Leadership Philosophy

I would suggest to you that one of the most fundamentally important things you can do to become an effective leader, manager, or supervisor is to think about, define, and then be able to articulate your own personal leadership philosophy

Your leadership philosophy can become the key to your effectiveness.

Your philosophy can be your true north. Everything you do, everything you say, every action, every decision, every plan should be driven by your philosophy. Your philosophy becomes your compass. It keeps you on track. It keeps you from straying. It is based upon a foundation of principles and values that are really important to you. It is the set of your sails. It becomes your true north.

Your philosophy can give you consistency. Without a leadership philosophy, your actions and your reactions will reflect the tensions of the moment. There is fear in the organization. "You never know what he will do!" "You never know what she might say!" With a leadership philosophy which you have carefully thought through, and which you know and understand, your actions and reactions are in synch with your philosophy. They are in context. They are predictable. There is less fear of the unknown in your organization. Your philosophy not only can become your true north, it also can give you consistency. Both have the potential to enhance your effectiveness.

Your leadership philosophy can connect you to your work. Your philosophy is all about your own personal mission and who you are as a leader, manager, or supervisor. If you are not clear on your own personal mission, your role as a leader will not be clear. If you are not clear on who you are, the people you lead won't be clear on what you are about. Your personal leadership philosophy must incorporate your very own personal mission. It must also incorporate who you are as a human being.

But then, if your own personal mission is in synch with AltaMed's mission, and who you are as a person is in synch with AltaMed's values, then your leadership philosophy will connect you to your work.

You can enhance your effectiveness by defining and then articulating your leadership philosophy.

So, let's do that. In order to craft an effective leadership philosophy I would suggest that you first carve out some time for inner reflection. You need to spend some time (months, not minutes) thinking about who you are and what you believe. Think deeply about who you want to be as a leader (not necessarily who you are right now.) Think about what you want your relationship to your people to be. Think about how you want to go about leading in an effective and transformational manner. Think about which principles and values are really important to you. More accurately, for each of these, don't think about who you are now or how you do things now, but rather, think about who you want to be and what you want your relationship with your employees to be, and how you want to go about getting things done. Design the kind of leader you aspire to be. And then live that design

How to structure your leadership philosophy. There are three components to a leadership philosophy. I will explain each in detail shortly. For now, just know that the first part is a statement of the principles and values which are important to you as a leader. The second part is a description of your overarching goals for your career – your desired results. And the third part is about how you plan to go about leading - your leadership style.

The three parts can be thought of as the three pillars of your philosophy. Think of the pillars as being the *why*, *what* and *how* of your leadership philosophy. The why is the principles and values. The what is your desired results. And the how is your leadership style. And you want them to be in this order - the why, the what, and then the how.

The first pillar or component is the *why*. Why you do what you do. Why you decide what you decide. It is because your actions are grounded in fundamental principles and values which drive you. The why pillar is basically a statement of what is really important to you as a leader.

Crafting Your Personal Leadership Philosophy

The second pillar or component is the *what*. Your bottom line overarching goal of what you intend to accomplish with your career, your desired results. The second pillar is about the *product* of your career.

The third pillar or component is the *how*. How you intend to go about making it happen. What you want your approach as a leader to be - your leadership style. The third pillar is about the process for achieving that product.

Three pillars, the why, what, and how of your leadership philosophy.

Let's look at each of the three in more detail.

<u>The first pillar – your principles and values</u>. Why is it important to include that first pillar (your principles and values) in your philosophy, and how should one go about determining which principles or values should become a part of your philosophy?

One of the definitions in Webster for philosophy is: "*A philosophy is a system of principles for guidance in practical affairs.*" Think about what principles or values are really important to you as a leader. Principles or values which can guide you in the practical affairs of leadership. Prioritize the three or four most important to you. The principles or values which drive you. The "vital few." This is the "why" pillar of your leadership philosophy.

These principles or values also become the foundation for your philosophy. They help you to focus on what is really important to you. You lead off your philosophy by describing the foundation upon which it is built.

Here are some examples of possible principles and values which you might consider for the "why" pillar: *honesty, fairness, transparency, justice, respect, compassion, patience, kindness, innovation, integrity, stewardship*. You get the idea. I am sure that you can come up with others which are even more meaningful to you.

Always be asking yourself this question, "Is this particular decision, this particular action, this particular plan firmly rooted in my principles or values of leadership?"

<u>The second pillar – your desired results</u>. For the second pillar think about your vision for what you hope your philosophy will enable you to achieve throughout your career, the "product" of your career? What do you envision to be your "body of work?"

There are a couple ways to approach this desired results component. Looking forward what would you say is your mission as a leader, manager, or supervisor? Your mission, if you can articulate it, in many respects will help you to describe your desired results – your overarching goal for your career.

Or you could think about what you would want your legacy to be at the end of your career. What would you want people to be saying about the results which you achieved with your career? This would be another way of describing your desired results - component two.

You can test this second component, or "what" pillar, of your philosophy by asking yourself this question, "Does this describe what I would like my legacy to be?" If it does, it is likely that you are good to go on this part of your philosophy! If not, you may need to work on your desired results component more.

Please note that we are not talking here about completing your annual objectives or leading particular projects. Nor are we talking about how high you hope to rise in the hierarchy of your organization. Your philosophy is about your overall impact on your organization, not your career. Although hopefully they are related to each other.

Here are several examples of "desired results" goals taken from actual personal leadership philosophies:

"build value by enhancing the loyalty of community, patients, and staff."

"lead an organization that is people-centered, improves population health across all socioeconomic classes, and is fiscally responsible."

"create a collaborative work environment where colleagues feel valued, respected, and highly motivated, and to continually improve patient outcomes."

Steven Covey said we should begin with the end in mind.[2] Component two, the "what" of the three pillars is essentially to describe the end which you have in mind.

<u>The third pillar – your leadership style</u>. The "how" pillar is all about how you want to go about being an effective leader. Think of it as the process which you intend to use in order to achieve the *product* you described in the desired results component of your philosophy. What approach to leadership do you need to use in order to accomplish your overarching goals? Can you envision a style of leadership that will make you maximally effective? Will you be more successful being autocratic or democratic? Being directive or empowering? Being top down or bottom up.

It is important to think about including the "how" in your philosophy so that you can be constantly reminding yourself, while in the heat of the battle, of what you have determined to be the best and most effective way to go about leading.

Here are some leadership style ("how" pillar) examples:

"My leadership style is primarily democratic spiced with elements of visionary leadership."

"My leadership style is based upon authentic relationships, a collaborative approach, and situational flexibility."

"My leadership style is to inspire and motivate others, to build alliances, and shared decision making."

"Involvement of others with extensive collaboration, using data to achieve strong results, and fostering strong relationships."

All are fine and help to describe the style which these particular leaders intend to use in order to be effective.

Succinct and all-encompassing. Your philosophy needs to be succinct yet all-encompassing. There are two key words which describe the objective of being succinct - clear and concise. Clear enough so that it can be helpful to you in making the decisions you have to make every day. Concise enough so that you can bring it to mind at any time, so that it really becomes a part of you. Make it 100 words or less.

For the most part your leadership philosophy is for your own internal use. Your philosophy needs to work for you while you are in the trenches fighting the battles.

Here is a suggestion which can help you keep it concise - you don't need to include explanations or examples in your philosophy. For example, you don't need to say "one of my important principles is justice because"… You already know the "because." It doesn't need to be in the statement of your philosophy. If you are sharing your philosophy with someone, you can explain. But for your use, your philosophy is to quickly remind you of who and what you are trying to be.

Although clear and concise is your goal, your philosophy should still be encompassing enough that it can be applied to every aspect of your daily activity as a leader. You should be able to *filter* every action, every decision, every response through your philosophy. You should be able to *apply* your philosophy to every issue, every problem and every opportunity. All encompassing.

You may have already noticed as a leader or manager or supervisor that from time to time you find yourself faced with a really difficult decision or a tough situation. When that happens, apply your philosophy. For any of these situations the question is: "How can my philosophy come into play here? How can it provide guidance for me in the practical affairs of my leadership?"

It is important that you spend some time crafting your first draft. It doesn't have to be sophisticated. Just be sure to include those three pillars. There is no doubt that your leadership philosophy will be a work in progress. It will change as you attend these sessions. It will change

Crafting Your Personal Leadership Philosophy

as you gain more leadership experience. It will change as you study and think about leadership. You need time to think about it, to grapple with it, to chew on it.

There is a deadline for development of the final version of your leadership philosophy. Everybody in this room will have a different deadline. To figure out what your own deadline is write the number 65 on a piece of paper. Under the number 65 put your current age. Now subtract. The number you have just calculated is the number of years you have to create the final version of your personal leadership philosophy. That would be your final version. You need a working version ASAP. Right now your goal should be to get started.

<u>Your leadership philosophy and your legacy.</u> Earlier I mentioned that you should think about your legacy when developing your philosophy. The reason it is useful to think about your legacy is that your legacy and your personal leadership philosophy in many respects are directly related to each other. They both have to do with who you are as a person and as a leader. They both have to do with how you relate to those you lead. They both have to do with achieving your desired results. Your leadership philosophy, well lived, will contribute to your legacy.

Here is the ultimate question. Ask yourself, "What kind of leader do I need to be in order to end up with the legacy I would like to leave?" And when you have determined the answer to that question, then take that answer and build it into your leadership philosophy.

Plan to have a working draft of your own personal leadership philosophy ready for our next session.

Your philosophy will flow the best if you use the following format:

My leadership philosophy is based on:

1. *My principles or values of* _____.
2. *My desired results (goals) of what I aim to achieve throughout my career are* _____.
3. *My leadership style to achieve these results is* _____.

Here are several "real world" leadership philosophies to give you the idea.

My leadership philosophy is based on my principles and values of mutual respect, honesty, integrity, and doing what is right; the desired result I aim to achieve throughout my career is to improve the lives of the people in the communities I serve; and my leadership style to achieve these results is to lead by example and to inspire creativity and a passion for change.

My leadership philosophy is based upon my principles of honesty, respect, fairness, commitment to excellence and innovation. My leadership goals are to create an open, respectful, collaborative environment in my organization centered on the main goal of providing high quality, safe patient care. My leadership style is participative, authentic and flexible.

In conclusion, let's go back to where we started today.

> *One ship sails east and another sails west,*
> *With the selfsame winds that blow;*
> *'Tis the set of the sails and not the gales*
> *That tells them where to go.*
>
> *Like the winds of the sea are the winds of time,*
> *As we journey along through life;*
> *'Tis the set of the soul that determines the goal,*
> *And not the calm or the strife.*

Today we began our first sailing lesson. How to set our sails—so that we are not victims of every gale that comes along, but rather so that we can steer our ship toward world class. Your leadership philosophy will help you do that.

What are we about here at AltaMed? The touch of the master's hand. People helping people.

Who do we, as leaders, managers, and supervisors, need to be? People consumed with unconditional caring. Caring hands and loving hearts.

Crafting Your Personal Leadership Philosophy

What do we need to do? Strengthen the web of love. Harness the energies of love.

And who do we do this for? Our friends and neighbors. Our colleagues and patients.

Ella Wilcox's poem asserts that it is the set of the soul that decides the goal, and not the calm or the strife. I am suggesting that for us, it is the internal set of our own personal leadership philosophy that decides the goal, and not the day to day events that confront us.

I encourage you to take the development of your leadership philosophy very seriously. It is an important key to your personal effectiveness.

Chapter Five

Leading Beyond the Bottom Line

> This challenging presentation points out that as leaders, we must focus on optimizing all four of our organization's major assets - tangible (financial), community, employees, and customers (patients). This lecture includes an in-depth analysis of each of these assets, as well as detailed suggestions for addressing them.

The Calf Path

One day through the primeval wood,
A calf walked home as good calves should;
And left a trail all bent askew
A crooked trail as all calves do.

Since then three hundred years have fled,
And I infer that calf is dead.
But still she left behind this trail,
And thereby hangs my moral tale.

The trail was taken up next day,
By a lone dog that passed that way;
And then a wise bellwether sheep
Followed the trail over vale and steep,
And drew the flock behind her too,
As good bellwethers always do.

And so, from that day, over hill and glade,
through those old woods a path was made;
And many people wound in and out,
And bent, and turned, and dodged about,

*And uttered righteous wrath
Because it was such a crooked path.
But still they followed--do not laugh--
the first migration of that calf.
And over this winding wood-way they stalked,
Because that calf wallowed when she walked.*

*This forest path became a lane,
That bent, and turned, and turned again;
This crooked lane became a road,
Over which many a poor horse with his load
Toiled on beneath the burning sun,
And journeyed some three miles for one.
And thus, for a century and a half
People followed in the footprints of that calf.*

*The years passed by with swiftness,
The road became a village street;
And thus, before people were aware,
A city's crowded thoroughfare.
And the central fact of the street was this,
It became the heart of a major metropolis;
And over that zig zag road there went
The traffic of a continent.
And now for two centuries and a half
People followed in the footprints of that calf.*

*Each day one hundred thousand people are led
By one confused calf near three centuries dead.
They follow in her crooked way
And lose one hundred years each day.
For thus such reverence is lent
To well established precedent.*

The Leadership Lectures

A moral lesson I might teach,
Were I ordained and called to preach.
For people are prone to go it blind
Along the calf paths of the mind,
And toil away from sun to sun
And do what other people have done.
They follow in the beaten track,
And out and in, and forth and back,
And still their dubious course pursue
Along the path that others do.
But how the wise old wood gods laugh
Who saw that first primeval path!

Many things this tale might teach,
But I am not ordained to preach.

Sam Walter Foss[1]

We are gathered here today…to talk about leadership. And we begin with a rather timely reminder. The importance of the open mind. Leadership is an art. Like any art, it requires flexibility and creativity. The way we did things in the past may no longer work. The way we thought about things in the past may no longer be relevant. The way we approached problems in the past may no longer be functional.

We all have a tendency to follow the well-worn calf path. And in doing so, we continue the zigs and the zags that may have gotten us to where we are now, but are not likely to get us to where we need to be in the future. Zigs and zags are neither efficient nor effective. We need to forge a new path, a leadership path. Hopefully, one that is straighter and more direct. Hopefully, one that will enable us not to have to lose one hundred years each day.

Keeping in mind the many things this tale might teach, let us think about a new leadership calf path. Leading beyond the bottom line.

Leading Beyond the Bottom Line

One of the most astounding things that ever happened to me in my career is that somehow in 1998 I ended up President of the American College of Physician Executives (now the American Association for Physician Leadership.) In 1998, the American College of Physician Executives had about 12,000 members—all physicians, and all of whom were (and most still are) leaders in health care institutions.

One of the things we did during my presidential year was to begin a conversation about the concept of leading beyond the bottom line. There is much emphasis in organizations, including AltaMed, on the bottom line. And for good reason. We have to lead to the bottom line, of course, but there is so much more that we have to be thinking about - beyond the bottom line. The concept became a four-day course offered by the College. It is also the topic of today's presentation.

In order to talk about leading beyond the bottom line, it is necessary to introduce you to the concept of the **four organizational assets**. These four assets not only constitute the bottom line but also enable us to lead beyond the bottom line.[2]

Here they are:

Tangible assets: Things you can see, touch, and feel - including financial assets. Most of them you will find on our AltaMed balance sheet.

Community assets: Our mission is to serve our communities. We are an asset to our communities. There is a flip side. Our communities can also be an asset to AltaMed.

Employee assets: You can read it on the back of our badges. Employees are our most valuable asset.

Customer assets: You can also read this on the back of our badges. Patients always come first. Our customers (patients) are assets without whom all the other assets become irrelevant.

Leading beyond the bottom line is optimizing all four of these assets—tangible, community, employees, and customers. A primary function of leaders, managers, and supervisors at AltaMed is to optimize these four assets.

I need to share with you two global considerations about these assets, and then we will explore each one. The first is obvious, if you think about it. These four assets are all interdependent. Not one can stand alone. You cannot maintain tangible assets without employees and customers. Customers are not customers without employees. And so on, interdependent. All four are important. Each of the four depends upon the others.

As leaders, managers, and supervisors, we must continually be aware of the importance of each—and the interdependence of each. No matter what our position at AltaMed, we must be aware of, and we must manage, all four. To lead beyond the bottom line, we must understand that these four assets are all interdependent.

The second global consideration of which we must be aware is that each asset has instrumental value. Instrumental value means that increasing the value of one increases the value of all. We can focus on one of these assets. In doing so, all four will be impacted. To lead beyond the bottom line we must understand that each asset has instrumental value.

Let's take a look at the four assets necessary for leading beyond the bottom line. For each of these assets I want to share with you thoughts and ideas that can be helpful for us as leaders, managers, and supervisors when it comes to enhancing that particular asset. For two of them (*tangible and community*), the ideas and comments will be brief. For the other two (*employees and customers*) we will explore in more depth three ideas relating to each.

Asset Number One: <u>The tangible asset.</u> We all would have to agree that the tangible is critically important. As they say, "No margin, no mission." We might also say, "No tangible, no mission." The tangible really has to do with leading to the bottom line. It will also enable us to lead *beyond* the bottom line. Remember, instrumental value.

Let me share with you your role in the tangible. After doing this stuff for 40 years, I have come to believe how important it is—no matter what your role - to know and understand and respect the financial, the tangible. No matter what your role at AltaMed - leader, manager, or supervisor - the more you understand about the budgets, the more you understand about balance sheets, and fixed costs, and depreciation, and cash flow, and capital budgeting - the more you understand all this stuff, the more effective you will be. If you want to increase your effectiveness, you must take the time to study and learn about finance and accounting. (Not at a Master's degree level, but rather at a basic level that is solid enough to enable you to be effective in your role.)

Here is another thought about tangible assets, and this should be regarded as a caution. As leaders, managers, and supervisors, we must be constantly on guard regarding the "inversion problem." Inversion occurs when mission is lost to financial considerations. Our leaders here at corporate do a pretty good job with this at the corporate level. You need to be continually alert to inversion at your particular level. The assets are all interdependent. Financial considerations can negatively impact the other three assets. They can impact the mission. Be alert for the phenomenon of inversion. And if you see it happening, don't stop yelling until it is addressed.

Leading beyond the bottom line. The tangible assets.

Asset Number Two: <u>The community asset</u> is one that most of us don't think about very often. We need to increase the loyalty of our communities. We need to make our communities an asset.

A very important community asset is the attitude of the community toward AltaMed. The community which has a positive attitude regarding AltaMed can become a very real asset. We need to nurture that.

We all need to get involved in managing the community asset. Not just our CEO and Vice Presidents, but rather all of us, as leaders, managers, and supervisors, have to work to influence community and business leaders. We need them to represent us, go to bat for us, defend us, and help us. We have to inspire them to "carry the water" for us. Image, brand, employer of choice, credibility, world class—building the loyalty of our communities. All of us need to get out there and help - via speakers' bureau, block clubs, little league coaches, PTA's, you can name it. The opportunities are there.

To nurture this asset, we should think about putting community requirements in nearly every salaried job description. We have done that for our providers. "Community contributions" are now included as an expectation in our provider performance evaluation system.

Here is another thought about why we should nurture our communities. Our communities house potential employees. How many of our providers grew up in our communities - and have come back? How many of our other employees have grown up in our communities? How many more potential providers or other potential employees are out there? Potential assets of AltaMed. The community attitude is so important. Nurture our communities.

Leading beyond the bottom line. The community asset.

Asset Number Three: Now let's explore the concept of loyal employees as an asset.

Allow me a disclaimer at this point. I have no HR credentials. I am not an employee expert. Our HR folks are busy helping us to create an "employer of choice" environment. My comments about creating loyal employees are mine alone - and, as they say, "Don't necessarily represent the views of AltaMed."

That being said, I was very pleased to discover when I came to AltaMed that our second value is that employees are our most valuable asset.

One of the first things I did at AltaMed was to go over to finance and ask for a copy of our balance sheet. Balance sheets, as you know, list the organization's assets and liabilities. If employees are our most valuable asset, I figured that I would find AltaMed employees listed on the asset side of the balance sheet. Not there. I finally found them. Employees are a line item on the <u>cost</u> side of the budget. Big difference.

So if not on the balance sheet, what does this mean - employees are our most valuable asset?

Herb Kelleher, Founder of Southwest Airlines: *"Employees come first. If you treat them well, then they treat the customers well, and that means your customers come back and your shareholders are happy."* [3]

AltaMed's first value: Patients always come first...*but* (I would add) *employees come more first.*

How do you develop a work force of fanatically loyal employees? Here are three thoughts. None of these thoughts is something that could be accomplished overnight. All will take a long-term commitment. Each will take a major focus. Every one, though, we can begin implementing tomorrow morning.

First thought: <u>Focus on what is really important to employees.</u> AltaMed has commissioned a major employee satisfaction survey—more than 60 questions. The survey will help us focus on what is really important. But only if we take it seriously.

We should decide to take the five highest dissatisfiers from our survey, and proclaim each one an emergency. Let's put everything else on the back burner until each of these five is addressed—not talked about, not planned about, but actually addressed, solved, off the list. Our most important asset - loyal employees. Do we actually mean that? Let's act like it. Let's walk the talk.

We say we want to be the employer of choice. Recently a major survey of 50 factors thought to be important to employees was administered to thousands of actual employees.[4] These thousands of employees identified what is really important. What topped the list? You could guess it. Not money. Appreciation. The number one most important employee satisfier - appreciation. I am guessing that AltaMed employees would say the same thing.

Employers (the bosses) also took the survey and predicted what they thought would be most important to their employees. Employers listed appreciation as number eight. Employees said that appreciation is number one. Big disconnect.

What do you do and say every day to be sure your people know how much you appreciate them, appreciate their work, and appreciate their effort? We do have some pockets of appreciation at AltaMed. Some of our leaders, managers, and supervisors are doing an excellent job with this. They should be commended. We can always do better.

We want loyal employees? Focus on what is most important. Appreciation. Every day. Your people can tell - the way you address them, the way you interact with them, what you say to them, how often you say, "Thank you." Appreciation.

What was number two on the employees' list of what is most important to them? Feeling in on things. How much trouble is it to help your people feel like they are in on things? Employers ranked this number ten. Employees ranked it number two.

Feeling in on things. Defining reality is a place to start. Staff meetings are good. Even better is the informal. The hallway conversations. Ask your employee's opinion about something going on.

When I first went to college, I would periodically encounter the president of the Student Association at the mailboxes. He would always ask my opinion about something that was going on. Almost anything. Did my opinion mean anything of consequence? No way. Did I, a lowly freshman, feel like I was in on things? You bet.

Ask your people their opinion about something going on. Will they feel like they are in on things? They surely will. Try asking your people what they feel they need to know about what is going on in order to do their job and be a part of this organization. You will be amazed at what you hear.

What was number three on the employees' list? <u>Help on personal problems.</u> Employers ranked this one number nine. Employees ranked it number three. We have EAP (a formal employee assistance program). That is a place to start. Even better would be asking your people periodically about how life is going. What are their dreams and personal goals? What are their personal challenges? And then, a key question - how can AltaMed help? We must recognize that if an employee has a problem, then the company has a problem, and it is to everyone's advantage to get it resolved immediately, before it becomes a customer problem.

The first thought for developing employee loyalty - focus on what is really important to the employees.

My second thought for developing employee loyalty - <u>selective and skillful hiring.</u> The fundamental question: Are we hiring the best people for the jobs which we have open? Are we putting the right people on the bus?

How do we get the right people? So often we hire out of desperation. Any body is better than no body. As is true in many companies, we hire quickly and fire slowly. Big problem.

We hire people for what they know. We end up firing them for who they are. It needs to be the exact opposite. We should hire people for who they are. And then worry about the "what they know" part later.

How do we hire the right people? Herb Kelleher, Southwest Airlines, again: "*Hiring starts off looking for people with a good attitude...that's what we are looking for...people who enjoy serving other people.*" [4] Would that hiring philosophy work for AltaMed?

Ed Ryan, published author on hiring the right people, says that the biggest reason why companies get stuck with the wrong people is that they base their hiring decision on a person's previous experience. *"This is a deadly mistake,"* says Ryan. *"Previous experience is a poor indicator of a person's future performance. The best is to look at their behavioral traits - who they are as a person, what drives them, how they make decisions, how they work and interact with others."* [5]

I often wonder if one of the biggest problems we have at AltaMed is not hiring the right people. It all starts from there. Although studies vary, if it turns out that the person we hire is not the right person, then it costs us 50-150% of their base pay plus 3 - 6 months of lost time. We need to take the time and do it right. As our VP of HR said at this month's General Management meeting, *"Our priority has to be the acquisition and retention of very competent people."*

Here is a suggestion for interviewing potential employees. Pick out two or three of your best people. What behavior traits about these two or three do you want to replicate? Take these attributes of your best people and don't be satisfied until you find them in a potential employee. Try this next time you have to interview a potential employee.

We must do a better job of interviewing. I think we need "just in time" interviewing training. You are getting ready to interview somebody. First you go over to HR to learn how to do it right. You say you don't have the time to go over to HR for "just in time" training? What are you thinking? A bad hire is going to cost you an inordinate amount of time. Hiring the right person is so important that AltaMed may want to consider a full time interview specialist.

AltaMed intends to become an employer of choice. As employer of choice, we will have people lined up at the door to choose from when hiring. FedEx has become an employer of choice. Our daughter (at the time a 40-year- old mother) saw that FedEx was advertising for several part time package sorter positions. She went over to Fed Ex to interview. There were 200 applicants for these several positions. Fed Ex spent several days triaging these potential employees. Their chances of getting the right employee were pretty good.

The second thought for developing employee loyalty - hire the right people - based upon their attributes, not their resume.

My third thought for developing employee loyalty - *extensive and unrelenting training and retraining*. Our mantra should be, "training and retraining - yesterday, today, and forever." Employees who are confident in what they do will like their jobs more, will be more loyal, and will provide an enhanced level of service.

AltaMed relies on front line employees to take responsibility. Training is essential in systems that rely on front-line employees to take responsibility. We cannot expect our employees to take front-line responsibility without adequate training. And by training, we are not talking about a single customer service class, though it is a good start. Rather, we are talking big time, never ending training. And when we are done training, the next day we begin retraining.

How many hours should be invested in training? Have you been to the Container Store? Their employees receive 235 hours of training in the first year.[6] Much of it is customer service training. Two hundred and thirty-five hours - that's one day short of six weeks. Do you allocate nearly six weeks for training of your new employees? What impact do you think that might have on your area of responsibility if you did?

After the first year, Container Store begins retraining[7] - they cut back though, only 162 hours per year. Four weeks and two hours every year - year after year. They believe that kind of investment will produce loyal employees...not to mention satisfied and loyal customers. Their staff turnover rate is less than 10%.[6]

Is the Container Store alone on this? Have you heard of Ritz Carlton, two time winner of the Malcolm Baldridge award? They provide 120 hours of customer service training during the first year and then 40 hours of continuing training per year.[8] One solid week of customer service training - every year.

The Dale Carnegie people say that every $1,000 invested in training will yield $4,000 from increased productivity and decreased turnover.[9] Loyal employees, delighted customers, strong and successful organizations.

Hewlett Packard, the computer hardware people, spent $275 million on training and retraining in 2005.[9] That figures out to be approximately one thousand dollars per employee. With eight hundred employees one thousand dollars per employee at AltaMed would be right around $800,000 budgeted annually for training and retraining.

How much money and how many hours do we invest in training each employee? Think what we could be. Do we want to become a Ritz Carlton in our communities? Do we want to become as successful as Hewlett Packard? We just have to decide to bite the bullet and do it.

As employer of choice, we will have developed a cadre of loyal, well trained, affirmed employees. Our turnover rate will be cut in half - or more. The quality of what we do will improve. It will be fun and fulfilling to come to work.

Leading beyond the bottom line. Employees as assets. Building employee loyalty. Appreciation, feeling in on things, help on personal problems, selective and skillful hiring, and unrelenting training and retraining.

These are places to start. These will make a big difference. And you can start with each one of these no matter where you are in this organization. You don't have to wait on the suits at Corporate. Apply these thoughts to your area of responsibility. You can do them. They are mostly all Steven Covey "Quadrant II" concepts. Important. Not urgent. But if you can make them work, they will change your life. If you can make them work, they will change AltaMed.

Leading beyond the bottom line. The employee asset.

Asset Number Four: Building customer loyalty. When we refer to customers, for the most part we are talking about our patients, or better said, our *guests*. Many of the examples which follow will relate to patients. For some of you, your major customers are internal customers. Colleagues whom you serve in one way or another. Some of these concepts will work for you also. Pay attention. Think about how what is being said could be relevant to your area of responsibility.

We want patients who are always satisfied. (We have met their expectations.) We want patients who are frequently delighted. (We have exceeded their expectations.) And we want patients who are occasionally dazzled. (Their expectations have been far exceeded.)

But most importantly, we want patients who are loyal. Patients who are satisfied may not always come back. In fact, studies show that 40% of satisfied customers will switch.[10] Loyal patients will always come back—even if the most recent visit was not satisfactory.

Financial statements have no ability to calculate the "lifetime value" of a loyal patient; nor can they calculate the cost of lost business due to a patient changing providers and never returning.

We have to be careful here not to confuse "repeat" patients with "loyal" patients, because there is a huge difference. Loyal patients will come back even when they have to drive further and wait longer. The repeat patient may change providers as soon as things become inconvenient.

Leading beyond the bottom line. It is patient loyalty that leads to improved profitability. Instrumental value. Do you remember? Any one of these four assets impacts each of the others. We want to get our patients to the door. And then, lock them in

The lock is loyalty.

I want to share with you three thoughts on creating customer loyalty. The three are interrelated. These three are meaningful to me because I think they are powerful contributors to loyalty. These three are also meaningful to me because they represent three of my failures at AltaMed. I tried to make these things happen. And they did not. It was my fault. If I could move the calendar back and start over at AltaMed, I would try again. Only this time I would try even harder.

It is not too late. In fact, as the saying goes, *"It is never too late to be what you might have been."* [11]

The first thought (and my first failure) is what I would call the "experience" factor. We need to turn our encounters into experiences. Preferably positive experiences. Have you heard of Starbucks? Starbucks turned a commodity (the lowly coffee bean) into an experience. Starbucks is beyond a beverage. We need to do the same. Starbucks' vision, by the way, is to develop enthusiastically satisfied customers all of the time.[12]

As opposed to Starbucks, in health care we have taken an experience and turned it into a commodity. The patient encounter. We need to turn our encounters into experiences. World class experiences. Renaming our patients "guests" would be a start. *Patient encounter vs. guest experience.*

When thinking about the experience that we need to create for our guests, we should think about both the environment to which we subject our patients and the interpersonal interactions between staff and guests.

What can we do with the environment in order to create a more memorable experience? Why is a fountain not in the plan for the waiting area at our soon-to-be-constructed center?

We started in this direction at another one of our centers. Four years ago we completely redid the waiting room - although not with a fountain. Nice furniture. Couches. Artwork on the walls. Fresh paint. A pleasing and comfortable environment. We are now back to rows of chairs (albeit nice chairs), five on one side of the row and four on the other - all looking out the door, not toward the center. That had to happen because the waiting room could not accommodate the patient growth. We grew the center - exam rooms and providers - without growing the waiting room. Bad planning. My fault. Efforts are underway now to expand the waiting room.

Look at the environment to which you subject your guests. Think about how you can make it more pleasant. Our patients actually asked for this during our World Class Encounter focus groups. They asked for a facility that is clean, safe, and soothing. Soothing - an interesting word, coming from our patients. Do you provide a soothing environment?

The environment. An important part of the experience factor.

The other half of the experience factor, and a huge one, is the interaction of the staff with the guest. Pleasant. Friendly. Professional. Interested. Did every staff member treat that guest as if she/he was our only guest? A study by the American Society for Quality found that 67% of customers who leave the organization do so because of the attitude of one person on the staff.[13] Patients are loyal because they somehow feel special when they visit your center. Do you do that? For every patient? Make them feel special?

Put on new glasses. Take a fresh look at the experience you are providing for your guests. And then get busy brainstorming about how you can make it better. Make it a Starbucks experience in the eyes of your guests.

The second of the three thoughts important in creating customer loyalty (and the second of my three failures) is to focus on managing expectations. So many times when there is an issue with a guest, we need to ask, "Is this a real problem or is this an expectations problem?"

Actually, guests don't care whether or not it is a real problem. If we did not meet their expectations, it is a problem - real or not.

Just as you should look around at the experience and the environment which you are providing, you should take a very serious look at the expectations of your guests.

What do they expect when they call? What do they expect when they walk in the door? How long do they expect to wait? In the clinics, which provider do they expect to see?

Talk with each other about our guests' expectations. Better yet, ask the patients about their expectations. Ask your guests. Conduct a few focus groups.

When you go out to dinner, what are your expectations? You are either satisfied, or delighted, or dissatisfied based upon - not the actual level of service and quality - but rather the level of service and quality which you were expecting.

Then, once you understand the expectations, you must manage them. Educate regarding appropriate expectations. Be alert to expectations. Deal with them in real time.

"Unexplained waits always seem longer than explained waits." What can you do about the unexplained waits?

Here is an example of what could be done. For this example, I have to draw on my pre-AltaMed experience. At each of our community health centers in Indianapolis, I had a full time greeter position. I tried to make this happen at AltaMed, but essentially failed.

The greeter was the friendliest, most outgoing person on our staff. If we didn't have a person like that, we went out and found one. The greeter did not sit behind a desk. She (or he) worked the waiting room. Greeted patients as they walked in the door, made sure the patient was appropriately registered, notified the back that the patient had arrived, chatted with patients who were waiting, often would go back to find out what was happening and then return to her/his "office"—the waiting room - to let everybody know. (Explained waits never seem as long.)

The greeter answered questions and offered fruit juice and healthy snacks. And when the visit was over, the greeter asked how it went, said farewell to the patient, and encouraged the patient to keep the return appointment. Hard work. Busy all day.

The greeter position. Managing expectations. Creating an experience. Worth the cost? Absolutely.

We had a policy, by the way that if short staffed - never pull the greeter. Too important.

Here is another example about managing expectations. It happened one Sunday morning. Our Sunday paper usually arrives about 8:00 am. On that Sunday morning we received a call from the delivery supervisor at 7:45. He advised us that the courier had not shown up for work that morning. They had implemented their back-up plan, but that we should not expect to receive the paper until 10:00. He assured us that we would receive our paper and apologized profusely for the delay. Managing expectations.

The paper actually arrived fifteen minutes "early" - at 9:45. We were delighted that it was early! Managing expectations. Instead of being thoroughly upset that our paper did not arrive on time, we were satisfied that our expectations were well managed.

As leaders, managers and supervisors, spend some quality time thinking about managing expectations.

Finally, the third thought…and my third failure. Develop a rapid response customer service recovery system.

When something goes wrong in the eyes of our guests, as it inevitably will no matter how good we get, what we do to respond and how soon we do it will ultimately determine our success. The better we are at this, the more loyal our guests will become.

Listen to these facts:

The average company loses ½ of its customers over a five year period.[14] At AltaMed we may lose more. We don't really know.

91% of dissatisfied customers never complain. They will simply leave and never come back.[15]

68% of customers who stop purchasing at a store do so because an indifferent employee treated them indifferently.[16] Big problem.

We must encourage complaints. If only 9% of dissatisfied customers complain, we have the other 91% out there telling others about their complaint and deciding not to come back. We need to make AltaMed easy to complain to. Patients need to know how to complain when they visit our centers.

And then, when we get complaints, we must have a system which will generate an immediate response.

When I first came to AltaMed, I had the idea that we should strategically place emergency call buttons in all of our AltaMed centers. Any employee who encounters a dissatisfied guest would press the closest call button, which would alert the nursing supervisor, the clinic administrator, and the site lead clinician. It would also alert the Vice President of Clinics at Corporate. At the time, that would have been me.

It turned out that apparently I was the only AltaMed employee who thought this was a great idea. (Which, by the way, is what happens to most of my great ideas!) In this idea, an employee who has been already trained and scripted on how to deal with dissatisfied patients, will receive immediate help - from the supervisors on the floor, from the clinic administrator, and from the Vice President, who is in his car and on his way to the site of this emergency.

Customers who have complaints resolved have a repurchase rate of 54%. When the complaints are resolved quickly, the repurchase intention rate rises to 82%.[17]

How long does it take to resolve a complaint at AltaMed? For many of the complaints, there are forms to fill out. The forms go over to the people at medical management, who already have way too much to do. In some cases the complaint has to be "leveled" for severity. The patient receives a call a few days later from medical management. By then, the patient may have called in the complaint to their health plan.

We should make it our target to resolve patient complaints in 30 minutes. A rapid response customer service recovery system.

We should empower our front line employees to be a key part of this system.

In my previous CEO life, I authorized every employee - every employee - to invest $50 of the corporation's money, if needed, to resolve a dissatisfaction. On the spot. Write off the charge. Movie tickets. Coupons to King Taco. A Target gift certificate. Whatever. Out of my budget. No questions asked. No one had to approve it. When it happened, I sent the employee a thank-you note. Make the guest happy. Build loyalty.

Some time ago while in Indianapolis, Barb and I offered to take our daughter, her husband, and their four kids - the triplets, then age 5 and big sister, Kelsey, age 6 - to dinner. They chose a restaurant named Bravo. Excellent casual Italian. There are two Bravo restaurants in Indianapolis—one 15 minutes from our daughter's house and one 30 minutes. We made a reservation for eight (four adults and four kids) at 5:45 at the closer of the two restaurants.

We arrived on time only to be told that a water main had broken a short time before and the restaurant not only was flooded, but it was closed. Four disappointed adults. Four sad kids. Although it was not their fault, customer service recovery was needed here.

The hostess of the closed Bravo told us that she had called our home number, but missed us as we were already on the way. She did not have our cell phone number. She also went on to tell us that she had called the other Bravo restaurant and reserved a table for eight, if we would be willing to drive up there.

We were and we did. And we were astounded at the reception we received. "You must be the Bensons. We are so sorry. Thank you so much for driving all the way up here. We want to give you complimentary appetizers." Before we left, the manager stopped by again to apologize and thank us. Will we go back to Bravo again? You bet.

A Bravo emergency? Yes. Was it Bravo's fault? No. Was service recovery needed? Yes. Was it immediate? Yes. Was it personal? Yes. Did the recovery include the managers, the wait staff, and the hostess? Yes. Did Bravo invest a bit of their corporate profit in the recovery? A bit. (A very good investment, by the way.)

At AltaMed we need to do in depth service recovery planning. We need a better plan than what we currently have. We need to train our people in service recovery and then drill frequently. We do fire drills. We need also to do service recovery drills.

Three thoughts toward building patient or guest loyalty: Create a memorable experience. Manage the expectations. Develop and practice an immediate service recovery procedure.

Finally, let me share with you about the recently developed AltaMed loyalty index. Here are the indicators which we are measuring.

Loyal customers make regular repeat purchases (visits). As already mentioned, there is more to loyalty than repeat visits, but this is definitely an important component.

Loyal customers will purchase across service lines. It is the brand that is important to the customer. Loyal AltaMed patients are willing to cross over service lines because the clinics, youth services, long term care and dental are all AltaMed. Loyal patients understand that.

Leading Beyond the Bottom Line

Loyal customers will refer others. Our marketing people will tell you that word of mouth is the best marketing. Loyal patients telling others about how great their provider is. They become advocates for bringing in new patients. We want apostles out there.

Loyal customers demonstrate an immunity to the pull of competition. It is six times more costly to get a new patient than to keep the one you have.[18] We want loyal patients.

Loyal customers can tolerate an occasional lapse without defecting. Loyal patients will give you more margin for error. First-time customers who are not yet loyal: no margin.

We measure satisfaction at AltaMed. We have now moved to the next level - loyalty. The loyalty index measures are based upon these five indicators.

Leading beyond the bottom line. The customer asset.

So there you have it. Broadening your focus as a leader or manager or supervisor beyond the bottom line. Understanding that we have four general categories of assets at AltaMed. We need to put time and energy into each one. These four assets - tangible, community, employees, and customers - are interdependent and instrumental. Enhancing one will enhance the others.

As a leader, manager, or supervisor, you can put emphasis on any of these four assets and you will be contributing to the others. But more importantly, as a leader, or manager, or supervisor, you will do well to be thinking about all four and doing what you can to improve each within your area of responsibility

Think about these suggestions which I have shared with you today. If they make sense to you, make them happen.

The **tangible** asset: (Enabling financial stability)

1. We must understand the tangible. We must understand about finance and accounting. We need more training in this area.

2. Be constantly alert for the inversion problem--when mission, at any level, is lost to financial considerations.

The **community** asset: (Building loyalty in our communities)

1. The attitude of the community and its leaders toward AltaMed is very important. We need to nurture a positive attitude.
2. All of us need to be part of managing the community asset.
3. Remember that there are potential AltaMed providers and employees out there in our communities. The community attitude may play a big role in whether or not they eventually become part of AltaMed.

The **employee** asset: (Developing loyal employees)

1. Focus on what is really important to your employees. Appreciation, feeling in on things, and help on personal problems are three that top the list.
2. Focus on skillful and selective hiring. Hire people for who they are. We need to continuously improve our interviewing skills.
3. Provide extensive training and retraining. How many hours are too many hours?

The **customer** asset: (Creating loyal patients)

1. Create a memorable and positive experience for our guests.
2. Manage the expectations of our guests.
3. Develop and practice a rapid response customer service recovery system.

And now, let's put this all together. I would propose this as our "leading beyond the bottom line" goal for AltaMed:

To help lead and support the creation of an organization which is world class in every way, with fulfilled employees, loyal patients, a supportive community, and a solid financial base.

To be an organization which patients seek out, which employees cherish, of which the community is proud, and in which financial stability becomes the "well spring" to do it all.

Is all of this a different calf path? Possibly. What we are about in our Leadership Development Institute is re-examining the calf paths of our minds. Open to new and better ways of doing things. Getting rid of the zigs and the zags. Making sure that we are not losing 100 years each day.

My hope is that the concept of leading beyond the bottom line will challenge some of your own personal leadership calf paths.

The result will be increased personal effectiveness as leaders, managers, and supervisors. And AltaMed will become a stronger organization.

Many things this tale might teach…but I am not ordained to preach.

Chapter Six

Embracing Change: Four Critical Concepts

> This lecture discusses the two types of external change, and the two distinct (and different) ways to respond. It shows how to manage obstacles to change and provides an introduction to two powerful change agents.

Alice

*She drank from a bottle called DRINK ME
And up she grew so tall,
She ate from a plate called TASTE ME
And down she shrank so small.*

*And so she changed,
While other people did nothing at all.*

Shel Silverstein[1]

The phenomenon of change. Shel Silverstein describing what happened to Alice…in Wonderland. It was time to change. She did what she needed to do. And so she changed. Other people did not do what they needed to do. And they did not change.

AltaMed is going through a time of tumultuous change. It is a good thing. The health care scene is changing fast. You have heard the following observation by Leland Kaiser in the first lecture and you will hear it again in the last: "Change in health care is happening so fast that

Embracing Change: Four Critical Concepts

it is difficult to look out our front windshield to see what is happening. Often, we have to resort to looking in our rear view mirrors - to watch the change going by. Change is happening that fast!" [2]

Do you remember the first fundamental task of an effective leader? Define reality. To be the leading community based provider of quality health and human services (our vision), we not only have to stay caught up with all of the changes, we have to get out ahead. If we resist drinking from the bottle called "drink me" and eating from the plate called "taste me", we will never see AltaMed's vision become reality. In fact, AltaMed, like so many other organizations, could very well cease to exist.

Chaos is everywhere. There is chaos at AltaMed. The greatest contributor to chaos is the one thing that is predictable in today's health care environment: change and its impact. As John Huey has said, "*The only constant in today's world is exponentially increasing change.*" [3]

Do you remember the very first lecture in this series...rediscovering fire? The second concept...in order to lead, manage, and work in our organization, you must embrace change. <u>Embrace</u>. What does that mean? Embrace means to clasp in your arms, hug, cherish, love. Embrace change. The Merriam-Webster dictionary also defines embrace: "to take up especially readily or gladly." Embrace change.

We must embrace change to enable our organization to survive in this tumultuous environment. We must embrace change to enable each of us to personally survive in this tumultuous environment. We must hug change, cherish change, and take it up readily and gladly.

The phenomenon of change. Let me warn you about what you are about to hear. You may have noticed that the title of this presentation includes the word "concepts." I am aware that you would prefer to hear a presentation about leadership and leading change that is more practical than conceptual. You would much rather hear that to manage change effectively, you must do the following four steps in a very particular order. You will not hear that today. I truly believe that you have to understand the conceptual in order for the practical to make sense. Hopefully these concepts will make sense to you and will give you context for dealing with the change which is happening all around us.

My objective is for you to be aware of the very different approaches to managing change based upon the underlying type of change and upon the role of chaos in organizational change. It is my hope that what I talk about today will become a part of the way you think, a part of both your personal and your management armamentarium.

Today I will share with you four important concepts that you must know in order to understand and successfully manage change.

The first concept is that a most interesting feature of change is that it is both the cause and the solution. Change is the cause of much of the chaos that we find all around us. But change also becomes the solution. External change is the cause. Internal change is the solution. You respond to change with change. You do not respond to change by staying the same. Always remember, and you have heard this from me before, *"If you want things to get better, you are probably going to have to change something."* The solution.

Concept number one: When dealing with chaos, remember that change is the cause, and change is the solution. External change is the cause. Internal change is the solution. External change is not optional. It is happening. Internal change is optional - depending upon whether or not you want to survive and thrive as an organization, and upon whether or not you want to survive and thrive as an employee.

The way to respond to external change is to change. If you don't change, you will not survive.

The second concept is that there are fundamentally two types of external change - linear incremental change and nonlinear discontinuous change. You have experienced both since coming to AltaMed, although you may not be aware of the difference.

Embracing Change: Four Critical Concepts

Linear change is change that is continuous and incremental. Plotting the change on graph paper looks like stair steps. Step after step after step. In the 80's and early 90's, most of the world was in an era of linear incremental change. I remember those days. You may not. Being a leader or a manager was actually pretty easy - although we did not realize that at the time. If you showed up for work each day and did your job, you pretty much knew that your organization would be there the next year and that you would still have a job.

Linear change is manageable. We can manage stair steps. One step at a time. The next step is fairly predictable. The change will be real, but it is not likely to be dramatic. There is not a whole lot of stress because you know the change is coming, it makes sense, you can plan for it, you can make a small incremental change to accommodate it, and you can live with it.

Examples of linear incremental change could be a new Joint Commission requirement or a new AltaMed procedure. Definitely changes, but incremental. Stair steps. Building upon what is already there.

The response to continuous incremental linear change is continuous incremental process improvement.

Nonlinear discontinuous change is dramatically different. This type of change as plotted on that graph paper is frequently discontinuous and chaotic. It may not be predictable. It is frequently a surprise. It is often so abrupt and so dramatic that it can knock you over. Much of the time we are not ready for it. In referring to nonlinear change, futurist Leland Kaiser says, "*The change these days is breathtaking. We don't need a pencil. We need an eraser.*"[2]

Examples of nonlinear discontinuous change could be a new organizational structure or possibly something dramatic like the State of California announcing a new payment mechanism or implementation of electronic medical records. Big time changes. We will have to do many things very differently. Not incremental at all. A whole new ball game.

Concept number two: There are fundamentally two types of external change - linear incremental change and nonlinear discontinuous change.

We are clearly in an era of nonlinear and discontinuous external change. Nonlinear discontinuous change creates a challenge for survival. We have to recognize it and respond appropriately. We have to know that if we continue to do things the way we did them, we will not survive. Just showing up for work each morning will no longer get it.

How do we respond to nonlinear discontinuous change? The response has to be <u>transformational</u>. Have you heard that word before? We have to transform the way we do things. We have to change the way we do things. We have to move from one paradigm to another--move from a paradigm of the past to the paradigm of the future. The response to discontinuous and nonlinear change cannot be incremental process improvement. By itself, incremental improvement is a prescription for losing these days. What got us to where we are now will not get us to where we need to be in the future.

Management guru Tom Peters says that *"the way to respond to such situations is to do something; in fact, do a lot of somethings, and do them fast."* He goes on to say that *"in today's world incremental change won't get the job done. The only way to keep up is to innovate and that means throwing out old ways of doing business and devising new ones."*[4]

Incremental process improvement is the correct methodology for incremental linear change. Transformational improvement has to be the correct methodology for discontinuous nonlinear change. Transformational. We have to be inventing solutions as we go. To be transformational, we often have to go where no one has gone before. Innovation and creativity. There is nothing incremental here in our response to discontinuous nonlinear change.

As we have just been reminded by Leland Kaiser and Tom Peters, unlearning becomes an important component of the transformational response. We have to learn, then unlearn, then learn again. That is what transformation is all about. We have to train, then untrain, then train again. As futurist Alvin Tofler has written, *"The illiterate of the future will be those who cannot learn, unlearn, and relearn."* [5]

On this same subject, Mike Vance, for many years the Director of Creativity for Walt Disney, in talking about the kind of internal change (the solution) that is necessary in responding to external nonlinear discontinuous change (the cause), affirms that we *"must make a conscious effort to clear the table; push the delete key; and start out fresh - if we hope to arrive at new and different solutions."* [6] This is not incremental. This is substantial change.

So we are in an era when transformational change is critical to our survival.

This is not to say that our incremental process improvement activity should be abandoned. Incremental improvements are also good. It is just that at this point in time, incremental by itself will not get the job done. The external change is, and will continue to be, big time. The response has to be big time, also. Transformational change.

<u>The third concept is that there are two major obstacles to transformational change—entrenched systems, structures, and processes, and entrenched mindsets of our people.</u>

James Belasco in talking about the two major obstacles to transformational change affirms that the first obstacle is the systems, structures, and processes already in place in our organization and the second obstacle is the mindsets of our people.[7] Both can cause transformational change to fail. Both must be addressed by the leaders, managers, and supervisors of AltaMed.

Obstacle number one is the systems, structures, and processes at AltaMed. The way we have always done things. Most of these systems, structures, and processes are well entrenched. They seem to be set in concrete. Many are covered with barnacles they have been around so long.

It is easier to keep on doing things the way we have been doing them than it is to change. *The way we are is a significant obstacle to transformational change.* Yet if we keep on doing what we have always done, we will keep on getting what we have always gotten.[8] We have to be willing, indeed anxious, to innovate, to blow up the systems, structures, and processes that now hold us back. To find a new path. The "entrenched systems, structures, and processes" obstacle. We have to get beyond obstacle number one.

Obstacle number two is the mindsets of our people. There are definitely barnacles and entrenchment here also. We definitely have "hard wired, over my dead body" people among us. There is so much fear of change. There is so much resistance from our people. *In so many cases, the traditional culture is more dedicated to preserving itself than to meeting new challenges.*

Let me say that again: "In so many cases, the traditional culture is more dedicated to preserving itself than to meeting new challenges."

We have to get beyond obstacle number two also. We must have a new mindset. A mindset that recognizes that the entrenchment and resistance are there and that AltaMed cannot respond to the need for transformational change if the people of AltaMed are not willing to accept the responsibility of changing.

As James Belasco said in his book, <u>Flight of the Buffalo</u>, "*I understand that I am the problem. Accepting that enables me to be the solution.*" [9] Each one of us must accept the responsibility for changing. Each one of us must be the solution. The "mindsets of our people" obstacle.

Concept number three: There are two major obstacles to transformational change—entrenched systems, structures, and processes, and entrenched mindsets of our people.

How do we respond to these two obstacles? Let's create a *culture for change* at AltaMed. A culture that addresses these two obstacles.

Embracing Change: Four Critical Concepts

So, here is our fourth concept: To create a culture for transformational change, two things are needed - empowerment and chaos. Just as there are two obstacles to change, there are two catalysts for change. We need empowerment to address obstacle number one - entrenched systems, structures, and processes. And we need chaos (with its associated passion) to address obstacle number two - the entrenched mindsets of our people. Empowerment plus chaos can lead to transformational change. Internal change that is transformational is necessary in order to respond to the nonlinear discontinuous external change that engulfs us every day.

Let's talk first about empowerment. To be able to successfully respond to nonlinear change, to be able to successfully respond to the need for transformational change, to be able to successfully break through obstacle number one (entrenched systems, structures, and processes) - we need to create at AltaMed an environment of empowerment. Our people have to believe that they are empowered to attack and break loose those entrenched systems, structures and processes.

What does this mean...this word "empowerment"? It simply means that we give to our staff the "power" to improve the things they work with. Empowerment. We recognize that staff know more about the processes that they work with than we as leaders do. We need our staff to help make things better, because the fact of the matter is that we leaders don't know how. If we knew how to make these things better, they would be better. But they are not.

So with empowerment, we empower our staff to be creative, to think about how to make things better for our internal and external customers. To do whatever it takes. We engage the minds of our people.

With empowerment, we are saying to our staff: "We value you. We respect you. We trust you. We need you."

Obstacle number one - the entrenchment of our systems, structures, and processes - exists because the staff would rather continue doing things the old way than have to deal with management's latest idea for improvement…an idea which they intuitively know is not likely to work. An idea which they are equally as likely to undermine. So obstacle number one continues to be obstacle number one.

With empowerment, we are saying to our staff: "You think of a better way, and we will do it." Empowerment involves the staff. They become important. Their ideas become important. And when the solution is <u>their</u> solution, the staff become committed to making it work.

Let me repeat: When the solution is <u>their</u> solution, the staff become committed to making it work.

You have heard me say this before. You are about to hear it again. *"People don't mind changing. They just mind being changed."* An empowered staff will lead the charge toward transformational change.

Empowerment sounds easy, but in reality it is quite difficult. To create an environment of empowerment takes several years. Empowerment is confusing. Both management and staff can misunderstand how empowerment really works. Empowerment can become quite emotional. Empowerment expectations by staff can far exceed reality. Yet, empowerment is very powerful. It not only delivers the combined intelligence of the entire staff, but it also invests the entire staff in the solution. Empowerment can become a critical component in the quest to respond to and manage nonlinear change.

Absolute leadership commitment to empowerment is essential. Leaders must talk the walk. But even more importantly, they must walk the talk. Leaders must open the door to empowerment. And then they must get out of the way. They must accept and support the results of empowerment. Leaders must be willing to invest the time and energy to help the staff understand empowerment, to inspire the staff to believe in empowerment, and to encourage staff to walk through the newly opened doors - to use this new found opportunity in a positive and creative way. Absolute leadership commitment is essential or empowerment will never work.

Embracing Change: Four Critical Concepts

As you know, at AltaMed if you have an idea to make things better, your idea is pre-approved. We call these ideas "pilots". Pilots do not have to be approved by management or the Vice President. You have an idea. Try it. If you need help in piloting your idea, I am ready to help. Before you begin your pilot, I want to know only two things: How will you know if your idea is an improvement, and how long will the pilot go? If it works, your idea becomes the way we do things. Empowerment.

To remove the systems, structures, and processes obstacle to transformational change, you must have an environment of empowerment.

What about obstacle number two - the "hardwired, over my dead body, we are not going to change" entrenched mindsets of our people?

In addition to empowerment, transformational change requires chaos and passion. Chaos <u>creates</u> passion. (I will say more about both shortly.) An environment of empowerment plus chaos is useful in creating transformational change.

Chaos is when things don't seem to be going well. When there is too much happening at once. When nobody seems to be really sure about what we are supposed to be doing. When the process is driving you crazy. When everyone is upset. When things seem to be a mess. Chaos is useful in creating transformational change.

This will surprise you: An important role of a leader is to <u>create chaos</u>. We think that the role of the leader and manager is to keep things settled down and under control. But truly transformational leaders do not believe that the world is orderly or that things will ever return to normal. That "normal" is past tense and will never exist again. The "new normal" is now.

Transformational leaders understand that there is a place for chaos in addressing the "entrenched mindsets" obstacle.

George Labovitz, a highly regarded leadership consultant to Fortune 500 Companies, in talking about what he calls New Leaders, says, *"New leaders continually focus on providing regular and appropriate doses of chaos. They push for 'stretch goals', frequently reshuffle their followers' roles and responsibilities, and openly challenge long-standing organizational assumptions. New Leaders thereby create unprecedented opportunities for innovation in responding to change."* [10]

As Socrates is reputed to have said, *"One of the responsibilities of leaders is to create the right kind of trouble."* [11] Socratic wisdom.

Why is chaos important in inspiring your staff to move beyond obstacle number two toward transformational change? Because chaos creates the motivation for transformational change.

Think about this. The primary result of chaos is destruction. Destruction makes reconstruction possible. Chaos precedes change and reorganization. Chaos makes transformational change possible.

You know from your zoology classroom days that caterpillars dissolve into liquid before becoming butterflies - a transformational change. The old and entrenched mindsets of obstacle number two have to dissolve into liquid before the transformational change can occur.

As futurist Leland Kaiser said when talking about chaos dynamics, *"Things have to fall apart before they can come together in a better way."* [2]

Is there any chaos at AltaMed? Do some things feel like they might be falling apart? If you are a smart leader, you might think about nurturing that chaos a bit, letting things fall apart a bit more. Why? Because chaos can become a powerful motivator in surmounting the obstacles to transformational change.

Here is something else about chaos - and this is the key. <u>Chaos creates passion</u>. Passion because the chaos is so unsettling that staff becomes determined to change things to make them better. As the saying goes, *"Change will not occur until the pain of staying the same exceeds the pain of changing."* [12]

With chaos, the pain of staying the same creates the passion. Staff becomes passionate about not having to live with this chaos any longer. Staff becomes uncomfortable. If staff is comfortable, there is little passion for change. Even empowerment is not very powerful if people are comfortable. However, with chaos the mindsets of the people become focused on moving away from the chaos and moving toward a better way - a transformational change. This reconstruction is not likely to happen without passion.

To remove the "mindsets of your people" obstacle to transformational change, you must have chaos, with its resulting passion, in your environment.

Concept number four: we can use empowerment and chaos as change agents.

Become a leader who skillfully manages both the linear and the nonlinear. Become a leader who understands and manages the two types of external change - incremental linear change and discontinuous nonlinear change. Become a leader who values the contribution that both chaos and empowerment can make to an organization.

Even if you are not officially a leader or a manager, you still encounter change every day in both your work life and your personal life. Here, too, you need to understand and manage the two types of external change, because they are happening all around you. You need to be able to manage skillfully both the linear and the nonlinear. Being able to manage this change in your personal and work life will make you more effective.

This is pretty scary stuff. As a manager, I suddenly feel insecure. Chaos is not comfortable. Should I really let that "fire" keep burning? If I am a skilled leader and manager, will I actually fan the flames on occasion? What will happen? Will my piece of this organization blow up? Will I get pink-slipped? How can I be comfortable dealing with the discontinuous and nonlinear changes that are occurring? Can I be comfortable with this empowerment thing? What if my empowered staff makes a bad decision? Can I really believe that the role of a transformational leader is to protect and nurture chaos? Does all this make me a bit fearful?

The Leadership Lectures

Parker Palmer, author, educator, and activist, focusing on issues of leadership, in a wonderful 1990 lecture on leadership entitled "Leadership from Within", suggests that all leaders have a shadow side (not "shadowy" side!). He describes several of these shadows—one, for example, being a leader's deep insecurity about her/his own identity, his/her own worth.

The fourth shadow which he describes relates precisely to the question of how we respond to our fear of stepping out and managing nonlinear phenomena in a new and dramatically different way.

Let me share with you this excerpt from his lecture:

> *The fourth shadow among leaders is fear. There are many kinds of fear, but I am thinking especially of our fear of the natural chaos of life. I think a lot of leaders become leaders because they have a life-long devotion to eliminating all remnants of chaos from the world. They are trying to order and organize things so thoroughly that the nasty stuff will never bubble up around us (such nasty stuff as dissent, innovation, challenge, change.)*
>
> *In an organization, this particular shadow gets projected outward as rigidity or rules, procedures, and personnel manuals. It creates corporate cultures that are imprisoning rather than empowering.*
>
> *What we forget from our spiritual tradition is that God created out of chaos! Chaos is the precondition to creativity, and any organization (or any individual) that doesn't have an arena of creative chaos is already half dead. When a leader is so fearful of chaos as to not be able to protect and nurture that arena for other people, there is deep trouble.*
>
> *The spiritual gift on the inner journey is to know that creation comes out of chaos and that even what has been created needs to be returned to chaos every now and then to get recreated in a more vital form. The empowering gift on this inner journey is the knowledge that in chaos I can not only survive, but I can thrive, that there is vitality in that chaotic field of energy.*[13]

Insights from Parker Palmer on the role of chaos. Insights from Parker Palmer on responding to the fear of chaos.

Embracing Change: Four Critical Concepts

The bottom line is that we need to create a "Culture for Change" at AltaMed. Not just incremental change, important as that is, but transformational change. Change that will enable us to adapt and move forward with confidence to achieve AltaMed's vision.

To create this culture for change, we have to understand the four concepts which I have just proposed.

1. External change is the cause, and internal change is the solution.
2. There are fundamentally two types of external change - linear incremental change and nonlinear discontinuous change.
3. There are two major obstacles to transformational change - entrenched systems, structures, and processes, and the entrenched mindsets of our people.
4. We can use empowerment and chaos, with its associated passion, as change agents.

You know that the traditional culture is more dedicated to preserving itself than to meeting new challenges. We must move our people beyond that. We must actively create a *Culture for Change* at AltaMed.

The culture for change that we want to create is:

- A culture where chaos is OK and well-led.
- A culture where change is accepted, valued, and embraced.
- A culture where ideas come through unhampered from people who previously would have been fearful about expressing them.
- A culture where people feel that they are empowered and at the center of things.
- A culture where the way we do things now is not OK.
- A culture where the vision is real and dynamic; where risk is encouraged; and where respect is the norm.
- A culture where the good of our patients and the community are number one.

The Leadership Lectures

Let me conclude with another Parker Palmer story from his lecture. This one describing his Outward Bound experience in northern Maine. It has to do with our fear of the unknown and our reluctance to step into the unknown. There is a message in this story for all of us. Don't miss it.

In the middle of the week I faced the challenge I feared most. One of our instructors backed me up to the edge of a cliff 110 feet above solid ground. He tied a rope to my waist—a rope that looked ill-kempt to me, and seemed to be starting to unravel—and told me to start "rappelling" down that cliff.

"Do what?" I said.

"Just go!" the instructor commanded, in typical Outward Bound fashion.

So I went—and immediately slammed into a ledge, some four feet down the edge of the cliff, with bone-jarring force.

The instructor looked down at me: "I don't think you've quite got it."

"Right," said I, being in no position to disagree. "So what am I supposed to do?"

"The only way to do this," he said, "is to lean back as far as you can. You need to get your body at right angles to the cliff so that your weight will be on your feet. It is counter-intuitive, but it is the only way that works."

I knew that he was wrong, of course. I knew that the trick was to hug the rope and to stay as close to the rock face as I could. So I tried it again, my way - and proceeded to smash into the next ledge, another four feet down.

"You still don't have it," the instructor said helpfully.

"OK." I said, "Tell me again what I am supposed to do.

"Lean way back," said he, "and take the next step."

The next step was a very big one, but I took it - and wonder of wonders, I leaned back into empty space, eyes fixed on the heavens in prayer, made little moves with my feet, and started descending down the rock face, gaining courage with every step.

I was about halfway down when the second instructor called up from below: "I think you better stop and see what's just below your feet." I lowered my eyes slowly - so as not to shift my weight - and saw that I was approaching a deep crevice in the face of the rock.

In order to get down, I would have to get around that hole, which meant I could not maintain the straight line of descent I had started to get comfortable with. I would need to change course and swing myself around that hole, to the left or to the right. I knew for a certainty that attempting to do so would lead directly to my death. I froze, paralyzed with fear.

The second instructor let me hang there, trembling, in silence for what seemed a very long time. Finally, she shouted up these helpful words: "Parker, is something wrong?"

To this day, I do not know where my words came from, though I have witnesses to the fact that I spoke them. In a high, squeaky voice I said, "I don't want to talk about it!"

"Then," said the second instructor, "it's time that you learned the Outward Bound motto."

"Oh, keen," I thought. "I'm about to die, and she's going to give me a motto."

But then she shouted ten words I hope never to forget, words whose high impact meaning I can still feel: "If you can't get out of it, get into it!"

Those words became so compelling that they burned into my mind, went into my flesh, and animated my legs and feet. No helicopter was going to come to rescue me; the instructor on the cliff would not pull me up with his rope; there was no parachute in my backpack to float me to the ground. There was no way out of my dilemma except to get into it - so my feet started to move and in just a few minutes I made it safely down.[13]

We began with Alice in Wonderland. We conclude with Parker on the cliff. The message from Alice…and from Parker…and from Dale: We are going to have to change - big time changes - in order to survive and be successful.

The secret is to understand and accept the fear, and then lean back and take the next step. Get into it.

> *"And so she changed,*
> *While other people did nothing at all."*

Chapter Seven

How To Be Effective When There Is No Time

> From time to time during the course of events, one runs across a book which has the potential to change one's life. One of those books, for me, is the late Steven Covey's <u>Seven Habits of Highly Effective People</u>. That book definitely changed my approach to life. If you have not read it, you should.
>
> The third of those seven habits has to do with effectively using your time. I think it is profoundly helpful. I have tried to pattern my activities around what I learned from that chapter. Much of this lecture was inspired by the Seven Habits book. I have not referenced every idea and quote from the book in my lecture, but I do it here in a general acknowledgment of appreciation to Steven Covey for his insight and excellent teaching.
>
> And so, borrowing heavily from Steven Covey, Harry Roberts and Aristotle, this lecture is not about how to increase your efficiency as a leader - rather, it is about how to increase your effectiveness as a leader.

Good Enough

My child, beware of "good enough,"
It is not made of sterling stuff;
Good enough is something anyone can do,
It separates the many from the few.
Its name is but a sham or fluff,
For it is never good enough.

With good enough the shirkers stop
In every factory and shop;
With good enough the failures rest
And lose to those who do their best.

Those who stop at good enough shall find,
Success has left them far behind.
With good enough ships have been wrecked,
The forward march of armies checked.
With good enough the car breaks down,
And those of high renown—fall down.

My child remember and be wise,
In good enough, disaster lies.
For this is true of people and stuff;
Only the best is good enough.

Edward Guest[1]
(Slightly modified)

Only the best is good enough. Today we once again talk about effectiveness. Only this time we are not talking about the effectiveness of a transformational leader. Rather we will be talking about effectiveness in our use of time. This will help you be more effective as a transformational leader. It will help you accomplish those five fundamental tasks of a transformational leader.

Do you remember the five tasks?

Task #1: Define reality
Task #2 Articulate the vision
Task #3 Create alignment
Task #4 Be a servant
Task #5 Say "thank you

How To Be Effective When There Is No Time

Have you incorporated these five tasks into your daily management activities? Do you think about them when you are driving to work every morning? Do you really want to be more effective? Is the problem that you do not have enough time to devote to these five transformational tasks?

Today's presentation is about our continuing, never-ending struggle with time. Time (or lack of it) is a huge barrier to effectiveness for many of us. Time can also be an enabler to effectiveness. It is all in how we use it.

Ultimately, today's presentation is about our struggle—caused by a lack of time—between "good enough" and "the best." You have heard that the enemy of the best is the good. This was validated in 1928 by Edward Gelt when he wrote the poem "Good Enough", a slightly modified version of which you just heard.

Only the best is good enough. Most of us, in the jobs that we do, whether leaders or managers or supervisors, are good enough. I would venture to say that very few, if any of us, are the best that we can be. In order to be the best, we need more time.

If only I had time enough, I could focus on the five fundamental tasks.

If only I had time enough, I could finish the first draft of my leadership philosophy.

If only I had time enough, I could focus on our vision for moving forward instead of constantly playing catch up.

Time is what we want the most and use the worst. We all start every day with exactly the same amount of time ahead of us for that day. How is it that some are successful and effective, and others barely get through their day—further behind than when they started…barely good enough?

Take a moment to consider your answer to the following two questions suggested by Steven Covey:[2]

What is the one activity that you know that if you did superbly well and consistently would have significant positive results in your personal life?

What is the one activity that you know that if you did superbly well and consistently would have significant positive results in your professional or work life?

And now, here is my bottom-line question for you: If you know these things would make such a significant difference, why are you not doing them now?

The difference between good enough and best is making the commitment and finding the time to do what is most important. As Steven Covey says, "Anything less than a conscious commitment to the important is an unconscious commitment to the unimportant."[3]

Today I want to present to you three concepts about how to be effective when there is not quite enough time. These concepts are not about time management, rather they are about "*myself*" management. These three concepts will enable us to move to the next level—from good enough to the best.

I can't manage time. But I can manage myself.

Much of what you are about to hear I have learned from others. Today you will hear ideas from Aristotle, Stephen Covey (big time), Roger and Rebecca Merrill, and Harry Roberts. These are not Dale Benson's concepts for effectiveness when there is not time. Rather, these are concepts culled from the writings of true experts in the field.

One final caveat before beginning the three concepts. And this will disappoint you. There is no magical, simple solution to effectiveness when there is no time. These concepts take understanding. They take commitment. They take prioritization. And they take a bit of a stubborn streak.

You will not hear magic solutions today. But you will hear a way to be more effective - in your personal and your professional life - when time is limited.

No magician ever pulled a rabbit out of a hat without first carefully putting one in there.

What we will be talking about is how to put that rabbit in that hat. Although they are not magical solutions, if you make these concepts work, it will be like magic. They will have a stunning impact on your life. They will have a stunning impact on your effectiveness.

What you are about to hear now is Steven Covey. **The first of the three concepts.** Here it is: *The main thing is to keep the main thing the main thing.*[4]

Covey divides every one of our activities into four quadrants.[5] The four quadrants are determined by asking two questions: *"Is this activity urgent?"*, and *"Is this activity important?"* The answers to these two questions determine which quadrant the activity goes into.

Covey defines "urgent" as requiring immediate attention. Urgent matters are usually visible. Urgent things act upon us. We react to urgent matters. Think about this: Everything we do is either urgent or not urgent.

Covey defines "important" as contributing to your mission, values, and goals. Contributing to relationships. Contributing to your health - physical, mental, social, and spiritual. Important things have to do with results. They require initiative. Important may likely be the two things which you wrote down at the start of this session that could dramatically change your personal and professional life. Think about this: Everything we do is either important or not important.

Let's look at Covey's four quadrants.

Quadrant I is for activities that are both urgent and important. Quadrant one activities are the crises that we deal with nearly every day - important and urgent. The fires that we have to put out - urgent, and often important. Pressing problems. Deadline driven projects. Last minute preparation - meetings, reports, proposals. Important and urgent, because it is the last minute. Urgent meetings are often Quadrant I.

Covey calls Quadrant I the "Quadrant of Crises." Many of you live in Quadrant I. Quadrant I deals with significant results (important) that require immediate attention (urgent). Quadrant I activities are often referred to as crises or problems.

Quadrant I consumes many people. Is it consuming you? If you made a list of everything you did this past week, how many items on the list would be Quadrant I activities?

As long as you focus on Quadrant I, it keeps getting bigger and bigger until it dominates you. The result - a life filled with stress, firefighting, crisis management, burnout. Is this your life at AltaMed? At home?

Quadrant III. There is another category of urgent activities. These are activities which are urgent, but not really that important. Covey places these activities in Quadrant III. Remember, urgent are things that happen to you.

Quadrant III includes many phone calls we receive, some meetings, drop-in visitors, some mail, some reports, many proximate pressing matters, and many popular activities. All urgent, but not really that important.

When we are in Quadrant III, we spend much time reacting to things that are urgent (assuming they are also important). But the urgency is based on priorities and expectations of <u>others</u>. Quadrant III results in short-term focus, feelings of victimization, loss of control, shallow relationships. <u>The voice of urgency creates the illusion of importance</u>. Urgent or not, they are not important activities. Places to go, things to do, people to see. Quadrant III does not contribute at all in moving us from "good enough" to the very best.

Quadrant I is the Quadrant of Crises. Quadrant III is the "Quadrant of Deception".

Quadrant IV. There is a category for things which are <u>neither</u> urgent nor important. It is Quadrant IV. How much of your time do you spend in Quadrant IV? Not really that important. Not urgent. It is there. You do it.

Quadrant IV. Trivia, busy work, junk mail, time wasters, some phone calls, procrastination activities, escape reading, escape TV, channel surfing. Even some sleep may be Quadrant IV.

Quadrant IV is the Quadrant of Waste. Of course, we really shouldn't be there at all. But we get so battle scarred from being tossed around in Quadrants I and III that we often "escape" to Quadrant IV for survival. Quadrant IV may have an initial "cotton candy" feel, but if we are interested in effectiveness, we quickly find that there is nothing there. Quadrant IV activities will not close the gap. It is the "Quadrant of Waste".

Which brings us to Quadrant II. Covey defines Quadrant II as activities that are not urgent, but that are important. Quadrant II activities are improving communication with people, taking the time to do careful planning and better organizing, seizing new opportunities, thorough preparation. Taking better care of self. Personal development.

Quadrant II activities also include crisis (or fire) prevention. Quadrant I (and sometimes III) is putting out fires. Quadrant II is preventing fires in the first place. There is no honor in spending your day putting out fires. There is honor in spending your day preventing fires.

Quadrant II also includes time spent in genuine relationship building. Improving communication with people. Our mentoring program is a Quadrant II activity.

Activities relating to our mission and values, time spent in clarification, understanding, and learning, and true re-creation (making things better), are Quadrant II.

Developing your own personal leadership philosophy is a Quadrant II activity. Important but not urgent. Even attending these Leadership Development Institute training sessions could be considered Quadrant II activity - important but not urgent.

All of the above are in Quadrant II. They are important. So why aren't people doing them? Why aren't you doing the things you identified back at the beginning? Probably because they are not urgent. They aren't pressing. They don't act on you. You have to act on them.

Quadrant II applies to your life at work. It also applies to your personal life. Read through the list again. All can relate to your personal life, also. Important but not urgent.

Quadrant II is the "Quadrant of Quality". It is the heart of effective personal management. It is not time management. It is "myself" management.

Quadrant II activities are high-leverage capacity building activities - in your personal life and at work. As already mentioned, Quadrant II deals with things such as building genuine relationships, long range planning, exercising, preventive maintenance, preparation.

If you will afford a gray-haired man the privilege of a personal example or two, I spend a portion of my time at AltaMed doing Quadrant II activities. Here is one: Our providers will tell you that at least once a year, about halfway between their annual performance evaluations, I schedule a personal "How is life going; and how is the career going?" session with each one - all of our providers. Relationship building, preventive maintenance, fire prevention. Important. Not urgent. Quadrant II.

At home I try to jog around the Rose Bowl every other day - 3.1 miles. Quadrant II. Important but not urgent. Both of these are important. They relate to personal goals. They are not urgent. They could be very easily postponed. Quadrant II.

How To Be Effective When There Is No Time

Quadrant II is the key. If you neglect Quadrant II, Quadrant I gets bigger. (If you neglect prevention, what happens to problems?) On the other hand, investing in Quadrant II will shrink Quadrant I. If your life is consumed by Quadrant I, you need to spend more time in Quadrant II. Covey says, "Effective leaders spend 50% of their time in Quadrant II." How much time do you spend in Quadrant II?[6]

Quadrant I acts upon you. You must act upon Quadrant II. Quadrant II, the Quadrant of Quality.

Here is a quick review of Covey's four Quadrants:

Urgent: Requires immediate attention. Urgent matters are usually visible. Urgent matters act upon us. We react to urgent matters.

Important: Contributes to your mission, values, goals. Has to do with results. Requires initiative.

>**Quadrant I**: Urgent and important. Deals with significant results that require immediate attention. Often referred to as crises or problems. Quadrant I consumes many people. As long as you focus on Quadrant I, it keeps getting bigger and bigger until it dominates you. Quadrant I is the *Quadrant of Crises*.
>
>**Quadrant II**: Important but not urgent. The heart of effective personal ("myself") management. High-leverage capacity building activities. Deals with things like building relationships, long range planning, exercising, preventive maintenance, preparation. Quadrant II is the *Quadrant of Quality*.
>
>**Quadrant III**: Urgent but not important. Much time spent reacting to things that are urgent, assuming they are also important. The urgency is based upon the priorities and expectations of others. The voice of urgency creates the illusion of importance. Urgent or not, they are not important activities. Quadrant III is the *Quadrant of Deception*.
>
>**Quadrant IV**: Not urgent. Not important. Totally worthless. Deterioration. Quadrant IV is the *Quadrant of Waste*.

Two questions for you: 1) During an average week, how much of your personal time do you spend in each Quadrant? 2) How much of your work time do you spend in each Quadrant?

So how does one move into Quadrant II? If we want different results, if we want to be more effective, we have to move into Quadrant II. We cannot keep on doing what we are doing. As the old saying goes, "If we keep on doing what we are doing, we will keep on getting what we are getting."[7]

If you are looking for time for Quadrant II, Quadrants III and IV are the places to get it. Effective people stay out of Quadrants III and IV because, urgent or not, these are not important. We need to be shifting more and more to the preparing, preventing, and empowering activities of Quadrant II. What percentage of your time is in Quadrants III and IV?

Quadrant II - Covey uses the phrase, "Putting first things first."[8] When urgency is the dominant factor in our lives, what we regard as "first things" are the urgent things. On the other hand, important tasks rarely must be done today—or even this week. They are easy to put off. What we should regard as "first things" are the important things. Putting the true first things first.

As Covey says, "The main thing is to make the main thing the main thing."[4]

We don't do the important Quadrant II things because they are not urgent. They aren't pressing. They don't act upon us. We must act upon them.

What is the difference between Quadrant I and Quadrant III? Both are urgent. Here is the difference: Did the urgent activity contribute to an important objective? If yes, Quadrant I. If no, Quadrant III.

To say "yes" to important Quadrant II priorities, you have to learn to say "no" to other activities—sometimes seemingly urgent things. Learn to say "no" pleasantly to Quadrants III and IV.

How To Be Effective When There Is No Time

As Goethe said, *"Things which matter most must never be at the mercy of things which matter least."*[9]

I am in charge of my life. How can I make Quadrant II happen? You must organize your life on a weekly basis. The way you spend your time ultimately is the way you see your priorities.

"The key is not to prioritize what's on your schedule. Rather the key is to schedule your priorities."[10]   Steven Covey

Let me quote Steven Covey again: "The key is not to prioritize what's on your schedule (that's time management), rather the key is to schedule your priorities."

Time management is really a misnomer. The real challenge is not to manage our time, but rather to manage ourselves. Organize your life around your priorities and values and mission. Then schedule around your priorities.

Here is a marvelous illustration of the four Quadrants concept. Imagine a large glass jar. You also have racquet balls, marbles, BBs (from your BB gun), and some water. First fill up the bowl with racquet balls. The bowl is full. Yet you can easily add a number of marbles until once again the bowl seems full. Now you can add many BBs to fill up the bowl. And when the bowl is full of racquet balls, marbles, and BBs, there is still room to add water.

What if you tried putting the four objects in the bowl in reverse order? It would not work. If the bowl was full of water and marbles and BBs, you could never get the racquet balls into the bowl.

Now consider that the water is Quadrant IV activity. The BBs are Quadrant III activity. The marbles are Quadrant I activity.

And the racquet balls are Quadrant II. The way to get the racquet balls into the bowl is to put them in first. Then the marbles; and finally the BBs and the water. You cannot get the racquet balls in if you first fill the bowl with the other objects.

The lesson: If you don't put the racquet balls (Quadrant II) in first, you will never get them in. If they go in first, it is amazing how many lesser things will also fit.

Quadrant II has to go in first.

Here is a suggestion. Go back to your office or cubicle, get out next week's schedule, think about your answers to those two "positive results" questions at the beginning of this lecture - *What activities if done consistently and well would have significant positive results in both your personal life and professional life?* Then build time for those activities into your schedule first. You will be able to fit everything else around them. Guaranteed.

"The greatest value of this process is not what it does to your schedule, but rather what it does to your head. As you begin to think more in terms of what is important, you begin to see time differently."[11]   Steven Covey

How to be effective when there is no time? Concept one. Build what is important, but not urgent, into your weekly schedule. Quadrant II. Make it happen. The Quadrant of Quality. Try it for a month. Let me know how it is working for you.

For concept number two on how to be effective when there is no time, I want to introduce you to the Harry Roberts checklist.

Harry Roberts was a Professor in the Graduate School of Business at the University of Chicago. Some time ago, I attended the annual meeting of the Institute for Healthcare Improvement in San Diego and had the opportunity to attend one of his sessions. He introduced his concept of the effectiveness checklist.[12]

Here is a very important distinction. The Harry Roberts checklist is not a "to do" list. Rather, it is a 'to be" list. It is not a list of things you need to do. Rather, it is a list of things that have to do with the kind of person you want to be.

How To Be Effective When There Is No Time

Do you remember those six concepts of leadership effectiveness which I introduced you to in our very first session…live our values, embrace change, respect, compassion, proactivity, and being willing to change yourself when necessary to change a situation? Some of these may be Quadrant II activities. Most of them are "to be" activities. The kind of person you need to be in order to be an effective leader. This is what the Harry Roberts checklist is all about.

How to be effective when you have no time? These Harry Roberts activities, for the most part, require no time at all!

First Harry Roberts told us about Bernie Sergesketter. Bernie Sergesketter was Vice President for the Central Region of AT&T. He originated the concept of this type of a checklist.[13] Not a list of things to do, but rather a list of things that would help him perform better.

At the end of every day, he would get out his list and count the "defects" – the word he used for the number of times that he did not successfully do what was on his list. His idea was that the defects could be friends, for they would inspire him to improve, to be more effective.

His list focused on three processes central to his work - meetings, telephone, and correspondence.

His "to be" checklist included items such as: 1) be on time to meetings; 2) answer phone by the second ring or return phone messages within one day; 3) reply to all correspondence within five working days (before the days of email).

His first month, he had more than 100 defects. He thought he had been getting to meetings on time; he thought he had been getting back promptly on phone messages; he thought he had been replying quickly to correspondence. The data showed otherwise. He kept at it and achieved a ten-fold reduction in his monthly defects.

Sergesketter discovered that meetings which started on time at AT&T finished 1/3 faster. (Did you hear that AltaMed? One-third faster. How much more time would we all have if our meetings were finished 1/3 faster?) He estimated that his personal time saved was about two hours per day.

Harry Roberts took this idea and made it a "personal quality standards" checklist. He calculated his defect totals weekly. And he plotted the points on a piece of graph paper. Microsoft Excel works just as well.

He developed four types of checklist standards: 1) Save time, 2) Eliminate waste, 3) Eliminate procrastination, and 4) Enhance personal attributes.

Here are the things he had on his initial checklist:[12]

1. On time to meetings
2. No griping
3. No unpleasantness
4. Not putting a small task on a temporary hold pile
5. Failure to discard incoming junk promptly
6. No unkind humor

For each item on the checklist, he also included his standard or goal for that item. He used the standards to determine at the end of the day whether or not he had any defects. And then, he added up the defects and plotted the points,

I don't use the checklist any longer, but I should. Here is the last of my lists which I could find.

1. Handle paper once—unless it will require more than 15 minutes.
2. Respond to memos or emails within 24 hours.
3. Return phone calls the same day.
4. Confront known conflict within 24 hours.
5. Read five journal pages per day.
6. Review memory 20 minutes daily.
7. Learn two new people's names per week.

How To Be Effective When There Is No Time

Let's look at the six concepts for effectiveness from our first lecture. Perhaps you could put them on a "to be" checklist.

1. Live the values.
2. Embrace change.
3. Respect for colleagues and patients.
4. Compassion toward colleagues and patients.
5. Be proactive.
6. Be willing to change yourself when necessary.

You might check off how you did on these at the end of every day.

You can make your own list. You know what could be on it. Start simple. Even one or two items, which you account for every day, can make a big difference in your life. One step at a time. Maybe add a few more items as you become better at using the checklist concept.

Here are Harry Roberts' tips for making the checklist concept successful:

1. Take it seriously. Give it a chance.
2. Keep it simple. One good standard can make a big difference.
3. Have clear operational definitions of checklist standards.
4. Use standards you believe in—not just socially acceptable standards.
5. Avoid activity expanders. Concentrate on waste reducers.
6. Don't try to change everything at once.[13]

I know this concept sounds a bit hokey. But I want you to think about it. It is really a substantial idea that will help you develop the leadership traits and habits that can contribute to your effectiveness - and it can help you eliminate those traits and habits that won't contribute to your effectives. And they take no time—except for adding up and plotting your defects at the end of the day.

The Harry Roberts checklist (the way you do things) is behavioral modification by the simple act of having the checklist in your pocket—or on your desk, or in your purse, or in your computer.

I challenge you to give it a try. One step at a time.

For concept number three, I need to share with you a short story. It is an Aesop's fable. (Here once again we are leaning heavily on Steven Covey. This time, habit number seven.[14])

One day a country man going to the nest of his goose found there an egg all yellow and glittering. When he took it up, it was as heavy as lead and he was going to throw it away because he thought a trick had been played on him. But he took it home on second thought and soon found it was an egg of pure gold.

Every morning the same thing occurred and he grew rich by selling his eggs. As he grew rich, he grew greedy; and thinking to get at once all the gold that the goose could give, he killed it and opened it, only to find nothing.

Concept number three is about maintaining the balance. Like the country man who owned the goose, we often emphasize short-term results at the expense of long-term prosperity. And in so doing, we destroy our capability for getting desired results.

Let's talk for a moment about true effectiveness. My definition of effectiveness is "the ability to change things for the better." Effectiveness is a function of two components—the production capacity (the goose) and what is produced (the egg). Long-term effectiveness lies in the balance between the two - the capacity (the goose) and the product (the egg). Neither without the other is effective over the long term. It is not just "the more you produce, the more effective you are". Effectiveness lies in the balance.

In order to be effective, you have to nurture the goose. If the goose is dead, you have no egg. In your life - personal or at work - you have to balance the nurturing with the producing. If you are too busy to nurture your production capacity, you will not be able to continue producing. You will lose your effectiveness.

Do you remember ever being too busy doing important things to stop and buy gas for your car? I do. What happened? It did not make any difference how many important things I had to do. I was not going to get there. I had squandered away my production capacity.

Will the pianist be able to continue to produce wonderful concerts (the golden egg) if she does not take the time to practice - to nurture the goose?

In order to be truly effective when there is no time, you have to invest time in the goose. And so, our discussion on effectiveness when there is no time concludes with the subject of personal renewal.

You now need to think about preserving and enhancing the greatest asset which you have - yourself. You are the goose. You need to be nurtured. You need to be strong. You need to be alive.

In order to be effective when there is no time, you need to take the time to invest in yourself. Taking the time to invest in yourself is the most powerful investment you can ever make in life. You cannot contribute to society, to AltaMed, to our patients, to your family, to your spouse if you do not first invest in yourself. You have to be able to produce those golden eggs.

Steven Covey says that the key to investing in yourself is personal renewal. And personal renewal is continuously renewing the four basic dimensions of the human personality - physical, mental, social, and spiritual. Covey calls it sharpening the saw.[15] Most all philosophies of life deal either implicitly or explicitly with these four dimensions.

Let's take a quick look at each one.

<u>Physical renewal</u>: Nutrition, rest, relaxation, regular exercise. Exercise is one of those Quadrant II high-leverage activities that most of us don't do consistently because it is not urgent. Regular physical renewal.

Mental renewal: Continuing learning (not necessarily classroom). Reading good literature (the best minds in the history of the world). Memorizing. Writing journals - thoughts, experiences, insights, learnings, ideas. Regular mental renewal.

Social renewal: Bless the lives of other people. Meaningful projects that are personally exciting and that contribute to the lives of other people. Be a positive scripter—an affirmer of other people. Family. Relationships. Random and unsolicited acts of kindness. Regular social renewal.

Spiritual renewal: Meditation, prayer, devotions, whatever works for you and is meaningful for you. Remind yourself at least once every day of what is really important to you. Regular spiritual renewal. The greatest battles in life are fought out daily in the silent chambers of the soul.[16]

These are all Quadrant II activities. Important. Not urgent. We must do them for ourselves. Organize your life so that you can continuously renew these four dimensions. Covey says that you should schedule one hour per day on personal renewal activities.[17] Keeping the goose healthy and strong - physically, mentally, socially, and spiritually.

You laugh. You say you do not have the time to invest one hour per day. How can you continue to be effective if you ignore nurturing your production capacity? You will be one cooked goose!

The essence of effectiveness is the commitment to balance the short-term with the long-term. Balance is the key. Excessive focus on production leads to ruined health, worn out machines, depleted bank accounts, broken relationships. Excessive focus on production capacity is not smart either. Three hours jogging per day can add years to your life. Then again, do you want to spend those years jogging?

Production capacity (the goose) vs. production (the golden eggs). The importance of the balance. Many people break themselves against this. There are people at AltaMed who are right now breaking themselves against this. You may be one of them. They do not keep the balance. They burn the candle at both ends. They can work with it. Or they can work against it.

How can I do this? One hour per day of "racquet ball" activity - Quadrant II. The importance of continual personal renewal.

Renewal is the principle - and the process - that enables us to move on an upward spiral of growth and change - of continuous improvement.

How to be effective when there is no time? Concept three. Maintain the balance.

In summary, these three concepts will enable you to be effective when there is no time. They will enable you to move from "good enough" to the best.

1. Steven Covey's Quadrant II. (The racquet balls go in first.)
2. The Harry Roberts checklist. (Not things to do, but rather, the way you want to do things, the way you want to be.)
3. A continual renewal of personal production capacity. (Nurture the goose.)

These are all difficult. They are all things that you need to do. There is no magic here. The magic comes when you begin to see the results.

How can I do this? One day at a time. One step at a time.

That which we persist in doing becomes easier...not because the nature of the task has changed, but because our ability to do so has increased.
Ralph Waldo Emerson[18]

How can I do this? One day at a time. One step at a time.

We are what we repeatedly do. Excellence then is not an act, but a habit.
Will Durant quoting from Aristotle[19]

For this is true of people and stuff. Only the best is good enough.

Chapter Eight

Twelve Tips for Leadership Effectiveness

> Each of these twelve tips is intensely practical, forged in the crucible of the real world. These truths became apparent over a lifelong career in health care leadership.

It Couldn't Be Done

Somebody said that this couldn't be done
But she with a chuckle replied,
That maybe it couldn't, but she would be one,
Who wouldn't say so 'til she tried.

So she buckled right in with a trace of a grin
On her face. If she worried she hid it.
She started to sing as she tackled these five fundamental tasks
That couldn't be done.
And she did it!

Somebody said, "You can never do that;
At least no one ever has done it."
So he took off his coat and took off his hat,
And the first thing we knew, he'd begun it.

With a lift of his chin and a bit of a grin,
If any doubt rose, he forbid it.
He started to sing as he tackled this personal leadership philosophy thing
That couldn't be done.
And he did it!

Twelve Tips for Leadership Effectiveness

There are many to tell you it cannot be done.
There are many just waiting to fail you.
There are many to point out to you one by one,
The problems that wait to assail you.

But if you buckle right in with a bit of a grin,
If you take off your coat and go to it,
If you start in to sing
as you tackle this effective leadership thing
That cannot be done,

You just might do it!

Edgar Albert Guest[1]
(Slightly modified)

And so, there you have it. You can do this. What do you mean "it can't be done"? Take off your hat. Take off your coat. Buckle right in. It can be done. Whether leader or manager or supervisor, you can survive. You can become effective.

When we began this series, it was playing the violin. The touch of the master's hand. Then it was Lester and his magic wish. Turning our wishes into reality. We followed this by learning to sail. It is the set of the sails and not the gales that decides which direction you will go. Before learning to sail, it was learning to fly. You do have more than eleven seconds. But the time has come. It can be done. By the way, upon hearing the poem about learning to fly, one AltaMed leader told me that she had no interest in learning to fly. Instead she wanted to learn to soar.

We then visited the calf and the crooked path and talked about creating new and more direct paths. Alice in Wonderland encouraged us to embrace change. And finally, we reflected on the concept that only the best is good enough.

They're all the same. Whether making music on a violin, or sailing, or flying, or following a calf path. It is about our effectiveness as leaders, managers, and supervisors. Effectiveness has to do with knowing how. And that is why we are here. Violin virtuosity, sailing, or flying do not come naturally. You have to work at it. Day after day. Month after month. Year after year. You have to know how. And that is what we are about in our Leadership Development Institute.

Today, I share with you twelve tips for leadership effectiveness. Each one of the twelve you need to think about. Some you should think about for the next month, others for the next year. And a few, you need to think about your entire career.

Much you have heard from me is conceptual. Concepts which are important to understand and to implement in order to be an effective leader, an effective employee, and an effective human being.

Each of these twelve tips is intensely practical. And each one is intensely personal, forged in the crucible of the real world. These tips are truths that have become apparent to me over my many years as a leader in health care organizations.

Some of them you might call Dale Benson's leadership principles. They have worked for me. I suspect that they might also work for you. Others are just tips. Things I have figured out over nearly four decades of trial and error. Trial and error, by the way, is what we call experience.

You may want to build one or more of these tips into your approach to leadership. It is not too late.

Tip #1. The first tip for leadership effectiveness is simply this: The Harry Roberts "To Be Checklist" is a powerful tool which can enable you to move toward achieving your vision of becoming an effective leader, manager, or supervisor.[2]

Twelve Tips for Leadership Effectiveness

Do you remember the Harry Roberts checklist - one of the techniques for effectiveness when there is no time? Even though it has not been that long since you first heard about it, I have put it first because it embodies so much effectiveness potential.

Here are quick reminders. You have heard of "To Do" lists. You probably use some variation of a "To Do" list every day. Harry Roberts said that we should also have and use everyday a "To Be" list. Not a list of things to do. But rather a list of things "to be", to help us toward being the kind of person, and the kind of leader or manager, we want to become.

Here are some examples: Do not procrastinate (do today's work today), arrive at all meetings on time, greet all colleagues pleasantly every morning, provide positive reinforcement to at least one co-worker every day, keep desk organized, return phone calls the same day.

You get the idea. Not a list of things to do in order to accomplish your job. Rather a list of things that will help you to be the kind of person (and the kind of supervisor, manager, or leader) you want to be. You don't need or want an extensive "To Be Checklist." Even one or two "to be's" will get you started.[3]

Harry Roberts said that you should review your list every morning and at the end of each day. Score yourself on how you did. It is all about developing the habits that will make you effective and successful.

The first leadership effectiveness tip: The Harry Roberts "To Be Checklist" will help you become the person that you want to be. It can help you to be effective as a leader, manager, or supervisor.

Tip #2. The second tip for leadership effectiveness is to focus your management energy on helping each of your people to achieve her or his potential. If you want your organization to achieve its potential, you have to be committed to helping your employees reach their potential. It is one of your most important tasks.

(Another important task!! Yikes! I thought there were five. Now there are six!)

An effective leader gets up in the morning and says, "What can I do today to make someone else better?" Making your people better is not only a task, but also a trait of leadership.

Here is a serious suggestion: At least once every year (in addition to the formal performance evaluation), sit down one-on-one with each of the employees for whom you are responsible and ask questions such as these:

How is life going?
How is your career going?
What would you like to be learning?
Do you have a career development plan?
How are you doing on it?
How can I be more helpful to you?
How can AltaMed be more helpful to you?

These one-on-ones are not performance evaluations. Rather, they are "How is it going?" conversations. Mentoring. Affirming. "Where do you see yourself in five years? In ten years? How can I, as your supervisor, be helpful to you in achieving your educational and career plans? How can AltaMed be helpful to you in achieving your educational and career plans?"

How often do you have conversations with your direct reports about their career development plans? Helping your people achieve their potential will help AltaMed achieve its potential.

By the way, here is a fringe benefit: When your people are progressing toward their potential, they can make you look awfully good.

The second leadership effectiveness tip: Everyday, focus on helping your people reach their potential. It can help you to be effective as a leader, manager, or supervisor.

Twelve Tips for Leadership Effectiveness

Tip #3. The third leadership effectiveness tip is to formally remind yourself each month what it is that you are supposed to be accomplishing.

Let me use a personal example to explain what I mean. Throughout my career I used a monthly tickler file. In that file for each and every month was a copy of my job description, my annual goals and objectives, my most recent performance evaluation, my current Harry Roberts "To Be" list, and a copy of my personal leadership philosophy.

On the first of every month, I re-read my job description (to be sure I was doing what I was supposed to be doing). I re-read my annual goals and objectives (to be sure I was accomplishing what I was supposed to be accomplishing). I re-read my most recent performance evaluation (to be sure I was improving what I was supposed to be improving). I re-read my current "To Be" list (to be certain that I was becoming what I wanted to be becoming.) And I re-read my personal leadership philosophy (to be sure that what I was doing and the decisions I was making were consistent with how I wanted to approach leadership.)

All five items. Every single month. Twelve times each year. Does this take some time? Certainly. Were there other items in my inbox at the time? Sure. Was it important to make this a top priority activity? Absolutely. It was well worth the time and effort. It kept me focused. It kept me aligned with my organization's priorities and with my personal priorities. A Quadrant II activity.

The third leadership effectiveness tip: Remind yourself every month what it is that you are supposed to be accomplishing. It can help you to be effective as a leader, manager, or supervisor.

Tip #4. The fourth tip for leadership effectiveness is to be extremely careful how you use emails. Emails can assist you. They can make you more efficient. As you know, they can also destroy you. Here are three email suggestions.

<u>Suggestion number one</u>: Never forget that the quality of your emails is as important as the quality of your other documents and the rest of your work. They send a message about how important quality is to you. Emails are not text messages written with your thumbs. Proofread and spell check each one. It will be worth the little extra time invested. People make judgments about you based upon how your emails look.

<u>Suggestion number two</u>: Never ever forget that any email you write could end up being forwarded to anyplace in the world and to hundreds or even thousands of people. Most important, it could also be forwarded to the person you are talking about in your email. Never ever send an email that you might regret the next day or the next month.

If you feel like sitting down and writing a sizzling response to an email you received, you can do it if it will help you feel better. But don't put the address in until you are ready to send it. If the address is already there because you clicked "reply", take it out before you write anything. (You absolutely don't want it going out accidentally. And you know that it can happen.)

Don't even <u>think</u> about sending it until you have had a day or two to cool off and consider very carefully about how it is worded and how it will be received. It is likely that you may decide that there is a better way to respond. (A better way, by the way, is a face-to-face conversation. A face-to-face conversation cannot be forwarded to others.)

Always think: What is the worst thing that could happen if I send this email? Because it could happen. Face-to-face or telephone conversations are always better if the situation is tense. Never conduct a battle by email. You will be asking for big time trouble. And it is very likely that you will lose.

<u>Suggestion number three</u>: Don't ever send what could be interpreted as personal bad news in an email. When you have to deliver news that is going to impact someone's life, or change someone's life, do the right thing: do it in person. Do not convey such information via email.

When I was a hospital Vice President in Chicago, I sent a job candidate an email saying he did not get the job. The address was incorrect and the email went to a random person, who wrote back and told me that he thought this was a pretty scruffy way of delivering bad news. He was right. From that point on, my policy became to always personally call and talk to anyone I have interviewed for a job and who did not get it. It is a huge issue of respect.

The fourth leadership effectiveness tip: Be extremely careful about how you use emails. Think about every email before you send it. It can help you to be effective as a leader, manager, or supervisor.

Tip #5. The fifth tip for leadership effectiveness relates to communication. Communication must be your top priority. If communication is not your top priority, all of your other priorities are at risk.[4]

Communication is always a problem in any organization. As one organization's supervisor is reputed to have written in an email, "*We know that communication is a problem, but the company does not plan to discuss it with our employees!*"

Lavish communication is key.[5] It is better to be guilty of over-communication rather than under-communication.

It's okay to communicate half the picture, if that's all you know. Say to your employees: "Here's what I know now. It's not complete, and it may change tomorrow, but I want to keep you in the loop." This builds credibility.

As you know, as a Vice President at AltaMed, I am responsible for all of the physicians and other health care providers. Each week for 250 consecutive weeks I have produced a two page update for the providers on what is going on and why. It takes a lot of time and energy. Every Thursday evening after dinner I sit down and type it up so that it can go out on Friday. I believe that it is important for the providers to know what is going on. Important enough to make it worth the trouble. Lavish communication.

Think every day about communication. "Do my people know what they need to know in order to do their job and to be an effective contributor to our mission?" Ask them on occasion for feedback on how you are doing in communicating, and what they feel they need to know that they are not hearing from you.

Take a felt-tipped marker and write the words "Lavish Communication" on a piece of paper or a 3x5 card, and put it above your desk, so that you are reminded every day to think about your role and your responsibility regarding communication.

The fifth leadership effectiveness tip: Lavish communication. It can help you to be effective as a leader, manager, or supervisor.

Tip #6. The sixth tip for leadership effectiveness is to utilize the power of concurrent feedback with your people. Here we are not talking about the annual performance evaluation. Rather we are talking about day to day in-the-moment feedback.

The technique that is most effective in changing performance (and is actually the most effective form of training) is concurrent feedback. Feedback once per year during the annual evaluation is of limited usefulness. Feedback that is timely - same day, same hour - has a much greater impact. The closer to real time, the better.

The feedback does not have to be negative or critical. Keep in mind that well-placed positive feedback can often improve performance more than negative feedback.

Feedback should always be respectful, with due consideration for privacy and confidentiality. If it is negative or constructive, it needs to be done in private. But it should be direct, honest, and timely.

Add this to your Harry Roberts "To Be" checklist: Give training feedback (or gratitude feedback) to my people often and as soon as possible.

The sixth leadership effectiveness tip: Incorporate the power of timely feedback in your management armamentarium. It can help you to be effective as a leader, manager, or supervisor.

Twelve Tips for Leadership Effectiveness

Tip #7. The seventh tip for leadership effectiveness is a series of suggestions regarding how to effectively accomplish employee performance evaluations. Know that I am keenly aware that I am not the Vice President of Human Resources. I am not an expert on performance evaluations, but I do have some experience-based suggestions. The fundamental principles you are about to hear may be worth consideration and could make our performance evaluation system even more effective. Learn from these principles.

First principle: Begin each evaluation with a review of the employee's life and career objectives - much like the midyear one-on-one conversation which I described earlier as "tip number two". Talk about how the organization can help in achieving these life and career objectives. Thus, this conversation becomes a semiannual event. It sends a strong and positive message to your employee - that you care, and that what happens to the employee is important to you.

Second principle: Don't even look at the evaluation form for at least the first 30 minutes. Discuss from memory your employee's strengths. Talk about ways to increase effectiveness.

Focus on strengths - not on weaknesses. Spend your time talking about how to make the strengths stronger. Weaknesses have a tendency to remain weaknesses, no matter what you say or do. Strengths remain strengths. So build on the strengths. Don't focus on the weaknesses. In the long run, focusing on improving weaknesses will not get you very far.

Third principle: An effective way to fill out the evaluation form is to do it together. (You should have already filled out a copy of the form prior to the evaluation session, so that the employee will know that you are taking this seriously.) Let your employee tell you what, in his or her judgment, the ranking on any given item should be. Tell your employee what number you put down. Often the two numbers are the same. You are in agreement.

Occasionally, the employee picks a number different than the one you chose. Sometimes it is higher. Sometimes it is lower. Talk about the differences. This will be good and useful information. You might even change your mind.

Fourth principle: Do the performance evaluation in the month that it is due. Even better, schedule it for the anniversary date. It is an important way to show respect. You can do this if you plan for it far enough in advance. On the first of every month, schedule your performance evaluations for that month.

The performance evaluation is an important management responsibility. You need to make it the priority that it truly is.

The seventh leadership effectiveness tip: Make the annual performance evaluation a high priority and a highly effective event. And make it happen when it is due. It can help you to be effective as a leader, manager, or supervisor.

Tip #8. The eighth tip for leadership effectiveness is to be aware that you are a mentor every day whether you want to be or not - in little ways and big ways. If you are a leader, manager, or supervisor, you are, *de facto*, an informal mentor.

If you are a parent, you know that your kids are watching you all the time. You are informally mentoring your kids. If you are a manager or leader, your "kids" are watching you all the time here, also.

What do you want people to see in you every single day, no matter what? What do you want your people to learn from you every single day, no matter what? Your integrity? Your actions? Your reactions? Your approach to problems? Your approach to people? You need to be sure to practice what you preach. Live your personal leadership philosophy. If you live your leadership philosophy, your people are likely to have a good sense of your philosophy without you even sharing it with them.

The eighth tip for leadership effectiveness: Never forget that you are always mentoring - for better or for worse. It can help you to be effective as a leader, manager, or supervisor.

Tip #9. The ninth tip for leadership effectiveness consists of four suggestions relating to interviewing and hiring. Once again let me issue a disclaimer. I am not speaking for HR. HR may have other approaches which, of course, you would follow. The HR suggestions are likely to be better. But it can still be useful to you to think about the basic philosophy behind these four suggestions.

First suggestion: Let the people who are going to be working with the candidate do the interview and make the selection recommendation. They know what the job entails. They know who will fit in and who won't. Plus, if you hire their recommendation, then they are invested in making their candidate successful.

Second suggestion: Remember the saying, *"We hire people for what they know, and we fire them for who they are."*[6] Spend your time in the interview finding out who they are. Their resume will tell you what they know. The resume does not always tell you who they are. Remember that the closest we ever come to perfection is when we write our resumes! You have to get inside that resume and find out who the candidate really is.[7]

Third suggestion: If you interview a good candidate and a position is not available, stay in touch. Email contact every two to three months ultimately can be rewarding.

If you interview two good candidates and can only hire one, stay in touch with the other. Again, email contact every two to three months can be rewarding. You never know when another opportunity may develop.

Fourth suggestion: As previously mentioned, always personally call those you interviewed and who did not get the job. Explain the reasons. They deserve that much respect.

The ninth leadership effectiveness tip: Think about these four suggestions when interviewing and hiring. They can help you to be effective as a leader, manager, or supervisor.

Tip #10. The tenth tip for leadership effectiveness relates to solving an interpersonal problem with another employee which is being experienced by one of your people. Studies have shown that 60% - 80% of all difficulties in organizations come from strained relationships among employees and the typical manager spends 25% - 40% of her/his time dealing with workplace conflicts.[8]

As a leader or a manager, we often get put between two employees who have some sort of battle going on. Instead of confronting each other, one of them comes to you and expects you to straighten out their wayward co-worker. Or sometimes they just are not happy with what another co-worker is doing…or not doing.

My policy was always this: If one employee came to me to complain about the performance of another employee, I would immediately volunteer to accompany the first employee to talk with the second employee. Together we would get the concerns out on the table.

What often happened was that the first employee would decide that the issue wasn't really that important, that we really did not need to go talk with the second employee. But just as often, when we did go ahead and meet with the second employee, the issue was dealt with and resolved.

The tenth leadership effectiveness tip: Don't accept the responsibility of solving someone else's interpersonal problem. It can help you to be effective as a leader, manager, or supervisor.

Tip #11. The eleventh tip for leadership effectiveness has to do with the importance of fire prevention.

We talk a lot about putting out fires. Problems occur frequently. Many are preventable. We call them "fires". It seems like every day the fires keep popping up. And they have to be put out. The problem needs to be solved. It is a Quadrant I or III problem - urgent, maybe important, maybe not. It takes time and energy. Time and energy that could better be invested elsewhere.

But it is even more important to spend time and energy on fire <u>prevention</u>. Every time you have a fire, and after it is put out, spend some time reflecting on the cause of that fire. Get serious about it. Think about what you could be doing differently that might have prevented that fire. And then start doing differently whatever that might be.

I have found that the one-on-one sessions with employees previously described become a very good fire prevention tool. Very often they give you an opportunity to be the smoke detector. Catch the fire before it actually happens. Just by listening very carefully to what your people are telling you.

I have always felt that managers who boast about spending their day putting out fires are actually not very effective managers. Your goal is not to be successful at putting out fires. Your goal is to eliminate the fires all together.

The eleventh leadership effectiveness tip: Make a point of spending a significant part of each day (or week) on fire prevention activities. Quadrant II activities. It can help you to be effective as a leader, manager or supervisor.

Tip #12. The twelfth (and final) tip for leadership effectiveness is a list of the most important phrases in the vocabulary of an effective leader and manager. They are also important and useful phrases for every employee - manager or not. Each one of these phrases could be the subject of an entire presentation. They are that important and useful.

So think about these phrases. Think about what they mean. Think about how they will impact your employees. Think about how much (or how little) you actually use these phrases. And then think about using them more often than you do. One or more of them could be candidates for your Harry Roberts "To Be" checklist.

Here are the phrases:

The <u>five</u> most important words for a leader or manager:

> *"You did a great job!"*

(Be honest. But be quick to praise. Praise is the most effective form of feedback.)

The <u>four</u> most important words for a leader or manager:

> *"What do you think?"*

(I need and respect your opinion. I will listen to you.)

The <u>three</u> most important words for a leader or manager:

> *"I was wrong."*

(One way to earn the eternal gratitude of those around you is by being willing to take blame. How broad are your shoulders? When you can do this, you will virtually never have to take all of the blame, because no one will ever let you. Apologies are always accepted, and graciousness counts for a lot.)

The <u>two</u> most important words for a leader or manager: (I could not decide between these three possibilities.)

> *"Thank you."* or *"I'm sorry."* or *"My fault."*

(All three are immensely powerful. Always say "Thank you." Every day. Saying "Thank you" is one of the five fundamental tasks. It is not difficult to say "I'm sorry" or "my fault." We really don't need to debate whose fault it is. But once you utter those words, the issue is behind us and we can move on. It is a very effective leadership or management technique.)

Twelve Tips for Leadership Effectiveness

The <u>one</u> most important word for a leader or manager:

"*We.*"

(We are a team. We are in this together.)

Memorize these phrases. Use them without hesitation. They will make a huge impact on your effectiveness as a leader, as a manager, or as a supervisor.

The twelfth leadership effectiveness tip: There are five phrases which can become an important part of your management vocabulary. Be quick to use them. These phrases can help you to be effective as a leader, manager, or supervisor.

Twelve tips for leadership effectiveness. My suggestion to you is to put these twelve tips in your tickler file - one for each month of the year. Tickle them in whatever order works best for you. You will be specifically thinking about and working on one of the twelve tips every month. If you do this throughout the entire year, you will have seriously reviewed and worked on each of these twelve.

My hope for you is that one or more (possibly even all) of these tips will be useful to you as you continue your quest to increase your effectiveness as a leader, manager, or supervisor at AltaMed. And ultimately my hope is that one or more (possibly even all) of these tips will play a small part in helping you to craft a successful and fulfilling career.

So that's it. As Edward Guest reminded us in his poem about how it couldn't be done, if you start in to sing as you tackle this thing that cannot be done, you just might do it. It actually takes more than singing, but you get the idea. Take your time. Think these things through. Make them a part of who you are. Make them a part of what you do. Make them a part of how you do it.

And then "*Start in to sing as you tackle this leadership thing that cannot be done. You just might do it!*"

Chapter Nine

Connecting the Threads

> This presentation summarizes the essence of what the author has learned about leadership over nearly forty years. It provides a high-level look at leadership at its most fundamental level. If you take all ideas, principles, and experiences regarding leadership and distill them to their purest essence, three fundamentals remain. This lecture discusses these three fundamentals.

Threads

Listen.

In every health care organization you hear the
threads of love and the threads of joy,
you hear the threads of fear and the threads of guilt,
The cries for celebrations and reassurance,
And somehow you know that connecting those threads
is what you are supposed to do…
And business takes care of itself.

James A. Autry[1]
(Modified slightly)

Today we will be talking about connecting those threads. This is not a lecture about the nuts and bolts of leadership. Rather, today I will be talking about the essence of leadership - boiled down and observed from 30,000 feet. A framework for leadership.

Connecting the Threads

I want to share with you three fundamental perspectives on leadership. Over the years, whether on purpose or by accident, I have learned much about leadership. If I take all of the ideas, and thoughts, and suggestions, and principles, and leadership experiences which have come my way, mix them together and distill them multiple times so that there is nothing left but the purest essence of leadership, these three fundamentals remain: 1) the importance of an integrated leadership philosophy, 2) the importance of an understanding of what really drives the people in your organization, and 3) the importance of an overarching responsibility to connect the threads.

First, you have heard me talk about the importance of having an integrated leadership philosophy. The time has come to share mine with you. Second, I want to reflect briefly on the essence of AltaMed. When you dig down to the very soul of our organization, what do you find? What drives the people of AltaMed? You need to understand this in order to be an effective leader at AltaMed. And finally, I will conclude with thoughts about our overarching responsibility as leaders, managers, and supervisors to connect the threads. What you are about to hear is a high- level view of the essence of leadership.

The first fundamental perspective: An understanding of the importance of an integrated leadership philosophy. Let me share mine with you. It is the result of more than 40 years of experience and more than 40 years of trying to understand what this leadership thing is all about. Much of my philosophy I have presented to you during earlier lectures. Only you did not know it at the time.

My philosophy as a leader is to be transformational, visionary, and supportive; to build value by increasing the loyalty of patients, community, and employees; and to accomplish this by "enlightened" empowerment.

Let's take a look at the pieces of this philosophy. The first three words are the basic values which I have integrated into my philosophy and which drive me every day.

<u>Transformational</u>. You have heard more than you want to hear from me about transformational leadership. Do you remember the five fundamental tasks of a transformational leader? Having endured several presentations on transformational leadership, I suspect you realize that there is much more to this word "transformational" than first meets the eye. The word has a whole lot to do with what I do every day. It has a whole lot to do with the way I try to be. It has a whole lot to do with the kind of results I hope to achieve. Transformational. From the paradigm of the past to the paradigm of the future.

<u>Visionary</u>. "Visionary" is a word we encountered briefly when talking about the five fundamental tasks of a transformational leader. Articulate your vision. Lead by the power of your vision. "Visionary" is a key component in my leadership philosophy because I believe that there is so much power in a vision.

<u>Supportive</u>. Supportive is key. Your people have to know that you are supportive. And not just in words. We have talked about that. Servant leadership - the fourth of the five fundamental tasks. Providing a supportive environment. Being present on the battlefield. Walking in the moccasins. Walking the talk.

Do you remember how surprised you were at that first lecture? Hearing about love, and respect, and caring, and compassion. Supportive.

Transformational, visionary, and supportive. This is my mental model for leadership, three basic values or principles which became the foundation for my leadership philosophy. The way I think about leadership.

The next phrases have to do with desired results – the product which I hope to achieve as a result of my career. Several months ago you heard me talking about this part of my leadership philosophy. Building value by leading beyond the bottom line. Do you remember the four organizational assets - financial, community, employees, and patients?

Connecting the Threads

My leadership philosophy is to be thinking all the time about how to build loyalty—of patients, community, and employees. (Financial somehow managed to escape my philosophy, but obviously it is fairly critical.) These are the ultimate outcomes which I am striving for.

At an earlier session, I proposed a "leading beyond the bottom line" goal for AltaMed. The goal I proposed was a reflection of this part of my leadership philosophy.

We are striving to build an organization which is world class in every way, with fulfilled employees, loyal guests, a supportive community, and a solid financial base.

An organization which patients seek out, which employees cherish, of which the community is proud, and with which financial stability becomes the "well-spring" to do it all.

Steven Covey advised us all to "begin with the end in mind."[2] The objective of the desired results component of my philosophy is essentially to describe the end which I have in mind. The overarching goal or "product" of my career. A key piece of the legacy which I hope to leave behind when I retire.

The final piece of my leadership philosophy has to do with process. How to accomplish this. The first part of the philosophy is my mental model – the fundamental values and principles which are important to me and which will drive my decisions and actions. The second part describes the desired outcome or result of my career, and the third part identifies the process. In describing the process I use the term "enlightened empowerment."

You know what empowerment is. Basically, it is the understanding that the people who work for you are likely to know and understand what they do better than you. Their ideas about how to improve things are likely to be better than yours. Empowerment means involving the people who work for you. Tapping into their brain power. Respecting and utilizing their abilities. Letting them play a pivotal role in the decision making and in the transformation of their part of our organization.

Empowerment is the understanding that no organization will be as effective as it could be if all the decisions are left to management. Empowerment is letting the decisions be made at the level where they are most relevant.

Enlightened empowerment is all about how to do that. Straight out empowerment is fraught with potential problems. Enlightened empowerment is a key to a stronger organization.

Enlightened empowerment involves decisions at the level of the action. But there is more to it than that. It won't work without the five fundamental tasks which we talked about in an earlier lecture. So be sure that you define reality, articulate the vision, and create alignment. The people whom you empower have to understand reality, believe the vision, and be heading in the direction that we are going.

If the empowerment is enlightened, we have to be willing to accept the results of the empowerment. Enlightened empowerment means first aligning our people, then unleashing their talents. Putting everyone in charge of something. Making our people feel as if they are at the center of things. The exponential power of empowerment. "How can I help you make things better?"

And so, there you have it. My personal leadership philosophy. If you have not done it yet, the time has come to think through and write that first draft. Sit down and grind it out. The way to get your first draft finished is to decide to do it. You will find it to be immensely helpful to you.

Understanding the importance of an integrated leadership philosophy. The first of the three fundamental perspectives that make up the essence of leadership.

The second fundamental perspective: An understanding of what drives the people in your organization. What drives the people of AltaMed? If you dig down to the core, what do you find? What is the soul of AltaMed?

Connecting the Threads

It has been said that you should ride the horse in the direction it is going.[3] You will be more effective as a leader if you ride the horse in the direction that it is going. We are talking here about the employee culture in an organization. The employee culture drives the people. What drives your people?

All organizations have an employee culture - a soul. Usually it is driven by top leadership. It may be a culture that is all about profit…or all about sales. Driven by the profit motive.

It may be a culture that is all about "me"…increasing my salary, moving up in the pecking order, owning more turf. Driven by the personal agendas.

It may be a culture of intelligence…great thinking, academic prowess, publishing papers. Driven by the mind.

It may be a culture of innovation…great ideas, great designs, always something new. Driven by the excitement of creativity.

It may be a culture of altruism…how in helping others, we are doing a good thing, making this world a little bit better. Driven by the heart.

There is nothing intrinsically wrong with any of these cultures. Every organization needs and has a sprinkling of each. Every organization has people who are driven by one or more of the above. The point is that every organization has a predominant culture - has its own soul. As a leader, you need to understand what that predominant culture is. And then get on the horse and ride it in the direction it is going. You need to do that in order to be an effective leader in the culture of the organization in which you work.

What if, in your view, the horse is going in the wrong direction? What if the predominant culture is not the culture you would like to see in your organization? Then your challenge becomes immeasurably greater. You have to turn that horse around. And turning a culture around, while it can be done, is a long and arduous journey. You need to hire a different kind of employee. You need to understand where that employee is coming from before you shake hands and say, "You're hired." You have to become a true transformational leader.

It can be done. But it will take a long time. It is better to ride the horse in the direction it is going. If for you the horse is going in the wrong direction, then you may be a leader in the wrong organization.

That being said, what drives the people of AltaMed? What is the employee culture of AltaMed? What is the soul of AltaMed? What direction is our horse going? You need to understand this in order to be an effective leader here. You need to ride the AltaMed horse in the direction that it is going.

I will share with you my answer. I believe it is correct.

The soul of AltaMed can be found in the heart of its people.

What is the soul of AltaMed? The soul of AltaMed is our reason for being. The soul of AltaMed is who we really are and what we believe. It is our mission, our vision, and our values. It is our people. It is caring, compassion, and commitment. It is our work culture. It is what drives the people of AltaMed. The soul of AltaMed.

To understand an organization, you have to touch its soul. We cannot understand AltaMed merely by looking at its balance sheet (important as that might be), or its statistical reports, or its promotional material. We understand AltaMed by looking into its soul. And the soul of AltaMed can be found in the hearts of the people of AltaMed.

AltaMed people have huge hearts. Hearts brimming with compassion and caring. And it is the heart of AltaMed people - their skill, their dedication, and their commitment - which makes AltaMed strong and effective.

What we do at AltaMed is very hard. There is so much stress. There is so much frustration. There are so many people in our communities needing help. And the resources are so limited. Yet the people of AltaMed are driven more by the heart than by the mind.

Connecting the Threads

The employee culture of AltaMed? We are driven predominantly by the heart. Profit is important. Personal advancement is important. Intelligence is important. Innovation is important. But my observation is that the predominant employee culture here is a culture of altruism, a culture of the heart. Our mission is genuine. Our mission is real. This is the direction our horse is going. The soul of AltaMed.

Throughout these years, I have taken great delight in experiencing and sharing the heart and soul of the people of AltaMed. Along the way I have encountered so many wonderful people here in this organization. Delightful people. People driven by our mission and our vision. Outstanding human beings. Talented. Passionate. Intelligent. Caring. If you look around this room, you will see a number of these people. If you look in the mirror, you will see another.

The second fundamental perspective: To be an effective leader, you must understand what is driving the people in your organization. You must understand the soul of your organization. The people of AltaMed are driven by the heart.

The third fundamental perspective: An understanding of our overarching responsibility to connect the threads.

What does this mean - to connect the threads? Ultimately, connecting the threads is about alignment. Connecting the threads is aligning the heart and the soul and the passion of AltaMed people. Connecting the threads is creating alignment by affirming, motivating, and inspiring your people. Connecting the threads is aligning the way we do things - the touch of the master's hand, the five fundamental tasks, strengthening the web of love. The little poem by James Autry with which I began this presentation describes the essence of this third perspective. Connecting the threads is something "that you are supposed to do."

Here is the key that you must understand to be an effective leader. Connecting the threads has to happen at two levels. The first level: helping each of your employees to reach her or his fullest potential. Align the individual. <u>The second level</u>: aligning your people so that your group or department or organization reaches its fullest potential. Aligning your organization.

Let me explain a bit more. The first level: Each of your people has to be maximally effective if your area of responsibility is going to be maximally effective. If one of your people is compromised, then your leadership effectiveness will be compromised. Your employee may be compromised by the stress of life, family problems, financial problems, interpersonal problems, or, as James Autry described, *"the threads of fear and the threads of guilt."*

If your employee is going to be maximally effective, if your employee is going to reach her or his fullest potential, the internal and external threads need to be in alignment. You are not responsible for their internal and external threads, but it would be well for you to understand where the threads are out of synch and be supportive. You need to understand where the threads are frayed and help if you can. James Autry again: *"Somehow you know that connecting those threads is what you are supposed to do."*

Here is a personal example. I have shared with you that with all of my 17 direct reports (and actually, in addition, with every provider), at least once a year I sit down with them one-on-one. The conversation is about how is life going? How is the family going? How is the career going? What direction do you want to go in life? Are you heading in that direction? I have several reasons for doing that, but a key one is that I am gently probing for disconnected or frayed threads. Not to be nosey regarding their private lives. But rather to be interested. To be supportive. And to understand.

Connecting the threads is what I am supposed to do. I cannot connect those threads at the individual level—but I can be supportive, I can be a listener. I can be interested. I can offer counseling and mentoring if asked. Or even an occasional and appropriate hug. The first level: Connecting the threads of each individual employee.

Connecting the Threads

Connecting the threads at the second level: Aligning your people so that your piece of our organization can reach its fullest potential. Here we are talking about the five fundamental tasks of a transformational leader - defining reality, articulating the vision, creating alignment, becoming a servant, and saying "thank you." Here we are talking about being sensitive to the dynamics in your group. As James Autry said, *"Listening for the cries for celebrations and the cries for reassurance."*

We talked about the three steps to creating alignment. First: Set the direction - everyone needs to understand where we are going. Second: Chart the course - everyone needs to understand our specific strategies, priorities, and objectives. And third: Talk the walk. You must be constantly talking the walk. As John Kotter has written, "Alignment is a communications problem, not a design problem."[4] Connecting the threads.

Connecting the threads is what your leadership philosophy should be all about. An integrated personal leadership philosophy will enable you to be more effective in connecting the threads.

The third fundamental leadership perspective: An understanding of our overarching responsibility to connect the threads.

The essence of leadership from 30,000 feet. Understanding the importance of an integrated leadership philosophy; understanding what drives the people in your organization; and understanding that an overarching leadership responsibility is to connect the threads.

I have one final perspective to share with you. It is so obvious that it doesn't even need to be said. But like other very obvious things, sometimes it is so obvious that we lose the perspective. The perspective is that it all has to do with people. And therein lies the challenge.

I have frequently said that the problem with doing quality assessment and improvement is the patients. If we did not have patients, we would have time to do all of this quality stuff.

The same could be said for leadership and management. The problem is that we work with people. If it wasn't for the fact that we are leading and managing people, this leadership and management stuff would be easy.

At AltaMed, we are people helping people. We are also people leading people. If you go to Barnes and Noble, you will find scores of books on leadership. The reason there are so many is that we are leading and managing people, and no two people are the same. Ultimately, it all has to do with people.

"It has to do with people" is the essence of what we do. And it is the essence of connecting the threads. It is the essence of leadership. Distilled down to the core. From 30,000 feet.

We are people leading and managing people. And our role as leaders, managers, and supervisors is to affirm, motivate, support, serve, and inspire the people in our organization so that they—in turn—will affirm, motivate, support, serve, and inspire our patients.

Listen.
In every organization you hear the
threads of love and the threads of joy,
you hear the threads of fear and the threads of guilt,
The cries for celebrations and reassurance,
And somehow you know that connecting those threads
is what you are supposed to do…
And business takes care of itself.

James A. Autry[1]

These three fundamental perspectives are the essence of effective leadership:

1. Understand and live your leadership philosophy.

2. Understand the soul of your organization.

3. Understand the critical importance of connecting the threads.

Connecting the Threads

And always remember - ultimately it has to do with people.

Think about these things - for the next five to ten…years. These concepts will serve you well.

Chapter Ten

Step Into It!

At the conclusion of most of the presentations at the Leadership Development Institute, we provided an opportunity for discussion. After that first presentation on the Rediscovery of Fire, two significant and profound questions were raised. Being one who needs time to think things through, I suggested that we could all think about these two questions and come back to them later. This gave me time to sit out on our fourth floor balcony in Pasadena during what seemed like summer evenings (they all seemed like summer evenings in southern California!) high among the palm trees and chat about them with my wife, Barb. She gave me some excellent ideas.

The first of the two questions was asked by Patricia Suarez, formerly the Director of Marketing for AltaMed. She is a very sharp and articulate professional. The second concern was expressed by Dr. Lloyd Johnson, the first physician I hired while at AltaMed. At the time, he was the director of the senior health care program and was highly respected by the entire staff. An interesting aside is that Dr. Johnson has a PhD in physics and worked in the nuclear arms industry for a number of years before deciding to go to medical school and invest the remainder of his career in helping people to be healthy.

At a subsequent leadership training session, I took some time and addressed these two questions. The response from the leaders, managers, and supervisors attending the presentation was overwhelming. It seems that a major nail was hit on the head.

Step Into It!

> At the end of each session, we asked people to write down and turn in what they were taking away from the session. We called them "take aways." I thought you might be interested in the reactions to what you are about to read. I have included some of the "take aways" at the end of this lecture.

You may recall that toward the end of that first lecture on the "rediscovery of fire", I suggested six concepts necessary as leaders, managers, and supervisors in order to move our organization toward world class. The sixth was that if you want to change a situation, you first have to change yourself. At that point, I shared with you a rather profound brief essay written in the 1950's by a San Francisco longshoreman who was also an author and philosopher, Eric Hoffer.

Hoffer's observation in relation to that sixth concept: *The remarkable thing is that we really love our neighbor only as much as we love ourselves. We do unto others as we do unto ourselves. We hate others when we hate ourselves. We are tolerant toward others when we tolerate ourselves. We forgive others when we forgive ourselves.*[1]

The point was that if we are going to love our neighbors more, or our patients more - or love each other more - we have to love ourselves more. Not in a pathological sense, but in a healthy sense. We have to change ourselves. If you want to change a situation, you have to be willing to change yourself. Patricia Suarez raised her hand and said, "How do we do that? How can we help someone - one of our leaders, managers, or supervisors - to love themselves more…so that they then can love our patients and colleagues more?"

What a good question. I have thought about this for a while now and still do not have a good answer. Here are three preliminary thoughts. First: We have to take Patricia's question very seriously. I am a firm believer in the notion that if you want your organization to achieve its potential, you have to help your people achieve their potential. If we want AltaMed to continue on its evolutionary axis of love and caring, we have to help each one of us to continue to grow and evolve on our own personal axis of love and caring. The first thought in response to Patricia's question about how to love ourselves more: we have to help our people do this. We have to take Patricia's question seriously.

Second thought: Obviously loving ourselves includes accepting ourselves for who we are. There are so many reasons that so many of us have difficulty accepting ourselves. Our heritage. Our background. Childhood experiences. Bad experiences. Unrealistic standards. Being told that we are not lovable or not capable or not worthwhile. All of these things we have to deal with.

I don't have many opportunities to watch Dr. Phil, but my wife, Barb, watches on occasion. Here are a couple of maxims from Dr. Phil which she shared with me. They address Patricia's question. The first relates to accepting yourself: You can't change what you don't acknowledge. You must acknowledge the events in your life that have contributed to you not loving yourself as much as you could. Acknowledge the history. Don't stuff it.

The second maxim has to do with what Dr. Phil calls "self-talk." The talk that goes on in your head every day. Talking to yourself. "I am so stupid." "I can't do this." "I am really worthless." "I can't do anything right." Constantly berating yourself. You have to change the tape.

The second thought in response to Patricia's question: You have to be willing to accept yourself as you are. Your "baseline." So that you can grow in acceptance from there.

Third thought: I do believe that the way we treat another can impact how that person accepts herself or himself. If I treat you as if you are truly worthwhile, truly lovable, and truly capable - in other words, if I treat you with genuine respect, you may begin to believe that you really are worthwhile, lovable, and capable. We may not be psychologists or counselors, but we can help each other to love ourselves more by demonstrating that each one of us is worthwhile, lovable, and capable.

Step Into It!

I am thinking that Patricia's question is a sentinel question. It is the bottom line of effectiveness. We need to come back to her question again and again.

How many people in this room truly don't love themselves as much as they should - for whatever reasons? Think about how that can impact your effectiveness as leaders, managers, and supervisors.

The second response came from Dr. Lloyd Johnson. After sitting through the presentation and hearing me talk about how we must internalize and live these six concepts every day, how we must harness the powerful energy of love, and how we must become the master's hand for each and every patient, he raised his hand and, in a very courageous act, confessed that he did not believe he could do this. That he did not have the character, or the energy, or the patience to make this happen. All of this is too much to contemplate in the face of each day's barrage of problems, issues, and frustrations - not to mention the barrage of patients.

As Dr. Johnson explained to me, "I think this is really important and I aspire to the challenging personal goals which you described, but I have a deep-seated fear that this requires more character than I have…or even more character than I have seen in others."

Again I have no answer. But I do have a thought or two. The first and most hopeful thought is the idea that courage to do all of this does not always roar like a lion. That sometimes it is a soft voice at the end of the day that whispers, "I will try again in the morning." The opportunity to "try again in the morning" has to be the beacon of hope for Lloyd Johnson, and for Dale Benson, and for every one of us really.

We fail in large ways sometimes, and in small ways often. But we can learn from our failures and we can try again. As the song goes, "I pick myself up, dust myself off, and start all over again."[2]

Just be sure to turn your failures inside out. How do you turn failure inside out? Have you ever pulled a shirt off a baby who has been sitting in a high chair eating crackers? The shirt can end up inside out.

What do you do with your failure? Just as with the inside out shirt, you...

1. Shake it. Not once. Not gently. But vigorously. Get all of the crumbs out.
2. Examine it. What happened? What does it mean?
3. Learn from it.

...and then, "try again in the morning."

I said I had a thought or two. The second is the concept of small steps. It was easy for me to write a speech about harnessing the power of love, and compassion, and respect, and proactivity, and rediscovering fire. Getting there overnight, however, is not possible. Getting there in a lifetime may not even be possible. But we can move in that direction. One step at a time. Even a small step gets us closer than we were. So think about where you are in all of this and think about what your next step might be. And then take a deep breath and step right out, and go for it.

There is a wonderful Outward Bound story (you may recall hearing it in an earlier lecture) about a student learning to rappel down the side of a cliff. Halfway down he panicked. He could not go up. He could not go down. He was hanging on the end of his rope. His instructor shouted up to him from below, "Step into it!" He did that and it worked.[3]

Step into it. That would be my suggestion to Dr. Johnson (who by the way has given me permission to use this example). That would be my suggestion to myself and to each one of us. We will not get to where we need to go if we decide that it is impossible. <u>We will be left hanging on the end of the rope.</u> We must step into it. We can harness the powerful energy of love here at AltaMed. Not by saying that it is impossible, but rather by stepping into it.

Step Into It!

But we have to be practical. Here is how to start. Make the small steps concrete. What is one practical concrete thing I could change about myself? It can't be, "I am going to love everybody who comes in." But it could be that I am going to work hard at making eye contact with everyone with whom I come in contact. Respect.

It can't be, "From here on out I am going to be proactive for the rest of my life." But it could be that I am going to try to be proactive for an entire day. Or a week. Or a month. Or maybe…for an hour!

What is one thing I could change to be more compassionate? What is one thing I could change to be more respectful? What is one thing I could change to help me live our values? Do one…and then another… and then another.

Here is a perfect example. And it came from observing Dr. Lloyd Johnson. You recall, the physician who said he could not do this? Two weeks ago, I was taking a physician we are trying to recruit around to see several of our centers and meet several of our providers. I thought we would get to Dr. Johnson's center around 11:15 or so. Dr. Johnson volunteered to arrange for lunch.

The lunch consisted of sandwiches he had made at home for us. He fixed and brought in our lunch. Truly giving. A small step, yes. But "stepping into it" none the less.

"Though no one can go back in time and make a brand new start, anyone can start from now and make a brand new ending."

Carl Bard[4]

* * * * * *

Two very profound and relevant questions. Both have to do with the rediscovery of fire.

The first question: How can people love themselves more, so that they can then love our patients and colleagues more?

- Don't stuff it. Accept yourself. Acknowledge the history.
- Change the tape. Delete the negative self-talk.
- Treat each other with genuine respect.

The second question: How can a person harness the energy of love and live those values-based concepts of embracing change, respect, compassion, proactivity, and being willing and able to change oneself when needed? Is this even possible?

- Turn failure inside out.
- Just step into it. Try again in the morning.
- Small concrete steps.

As discussed previously, if one or more of your people are compromised, your leadership effectiveness will be compromised. Do you remember about the importance of connecting the threads? Hopefully, these thoughts, ideas, and suggestions will be helpful to you in connecting those threads, and as a result, enable you to become a stronger and more successful leader.

Selected "Take Aways"

from AltaMed's Leaders, Managers, and Supervisors

"I will try again in the morning." Every day I walk the same path and fall in the same place. Tomorrow morning, I will try to choose another path.

The example used by Dr. Benson regarding the little step taken by Dr. Johnson was very endearing and gave me a different perspective about one's ability to make even the smallest changes.

Powerful thoughts - I can't emphasize enough how scary the thought of acknowledging self is. I must accept myself and somehow facilitate changing the tape.

Step Into It!

I need to change the tape, the negativity that I am constantly telling myself. I need to work it into a positive tape that will help me to better myself and to strive for my best.

I need to acknowledge the areas that need change by changing attitudes about myself. I can do this by starting with self-talk and trying again in the morning.

Self-talk. It is so important that I change the tape to positive self-talk.

"You have to change the tape." The self-talk or conversations in our head can often be debilitating. When changing the tape, we can begin by thinking about small steps and remembering that there is always a morning of new beginnings and hope.

Changing yourself, one step at a time. It seems easier to do when you think about it in that way.

Acknowledge the history and change the tape. I think this is very important in our professional and personal lives. It is certainly crucial in my life.

Taking small steps to change. It's all about small steps. I have started to do this by thanking my assistants when they do the things they do every day. Just giving a simple thank you.

I must accept failure as a way of learning. I should not consider myself to be a worthless person. I have to remember that there is a tomorrow and I can try again.

I'll try again tomorrow. It's OK!

Chapter Eleven

Eight Rules for a Fulfilling Career

> This lecture presents the author's eight rules for a fulfilling career. These rules become a guidepost for leaders, managers, and supervisors, as well as providers and other health care professionals.

Leadership

Leaders are called to stand in that lonely place
between the no longer and the not yet
and intentionally make decisions
that will bind, forge, move
and create history.

We are not called to be popular,
we are not called to be safe,
we are not called to follow,
we are the ones called to take risks,
we are the ones called to change attitudes;
to risk displeasures,
we are the ones called to gamble our lives,
for a better world.

Mary Lou Andersen[1]

Making a better world. That's what we are about. How do we do that? We begin with where we are right now - at AltaMed Health Services in East Los Angeles. One day at a time. One hour at a time. One patient at a time. As leadership expert Tom Peters has challenged us, "Excellence (as leaders) is not an aspiration. Rather it is what you do in the next five minutes."[2]

I really like the opening thought of this wonderful little poem about leadership written by Mary Lou Anderson. "Leaders are called to stand in that lonely place between the no-longer and the not-yet." As transformational leaders, and everyone in this room is a leader no matter what your role at AltaMed, as you help to move AltaMed from the paradigm of the past (yesterday) toward the paradigm of the future (tomorrow), you will often find yourselves standing in that lonely place between the no-longer and the not-yet.

There is a lot of pain out there right now. Big time changes are happening to the structure of medicine. These changes are impacting the way we practice. That hurts.

But here is a concept that is important to remember in the midst of all of this pain and change: *although pain is inevitable, misery is optional.* As Steven Covey has pointed out, we have the ability to choose how we respond to a situation.[3] If we choose to respond to all of this change with low morale, we will have low morale. Guaranteed. If we choose to remain positive and committed to making it work, we can make a difference.

Here is something else: In spite of the chaos out there, one extremely important element remains, one which we should never forget. We as health care professionals are privileged to share in the care of those who are sick, scared, and vulnerable. Many of us who are providers are privileged to share in the intimacy of the exam room. And that has not changed! *The structure of medicine may be changing, but the opportunity to bring healing to the lives of others has not changed.* And with that comes the possibility of a career filled with joy, fulfillment, and deep internal satisfaction.

That being said, I want to share with you Benson's eight rules for a fulfilling career. These rules are not necessarily profound, but I am hopeful that they will be thought-provoking. Take them with you, and make them a part of everything you do. They can become a foundation of support for you as you encounter these never-ending winds of change.

Rule #1: Be proud of what you are doing. No matter what your role, you are impacting people's lives. At AltaMed you all share in that privilege of caring for people when they are sick, scared, and vulnerable. Many of you share in that intimacy of the exam room. For your patients, AltaMed is a locus of hope and support in a chaotic world. You are touching the body, mind, and spirit of other human beings. Be proud of what you are doing.

Oliver Wendell Holmes, *"Every calling is great when greatly pursued."*[4] Your calling is great and is to be greatly pursued. Be proud of your calling. Pursue it greatly.

Marcia Ann Gillespie - a trailblazer in the magazine industry, a leader in the women's movement, and an activist for gender and racial justice, *"Part of true success is understanding that there is something bigger and more important than ourselves."*[5] You are part of something bigger and more important. AltaMed is part of something bigger and more important. Be proud of what you are doing.

But be proud in a positive sense, not in a negative egotistical sense. You are devoting your career to the well-being of others. You are making a difference. Be proud of that.

Rule #1 for a fulfilling career: Be proud of what you are doing.

Rule #2. Be humble that you have this privilege. Be proud in a humble sort of way. Here I quote John Ruskin, 19th century English critic of art, architecture and society, *"The first test of a truly great man (or woman) is his (or her) humility."*[6] Be humble that you have this privilege.

Leadership is not a trumpet call to self-importance – rather, it is an opportunity to serve. Become a servant leader. Walk the talk. As observed by Laozi several thousand years ago, *"The good leader carries water for his (or her) people."*[7] Be humble enough to carry the water for your people. As has been said, *"If serving is beneath you, then leading is beyond you."*[8]

God has given you your talent, your intelligence, your motivation, your ability to interact with patients. To care for people who are sick, scared, and vulnerable is a sacred privilege. Be humble that you have that privilege. To be a provider at AltaMed is a sacred privilege. Be humble in your interactions with patients and staff.

Here is the question - how does rule number two (be humble) relate to rule number one (be proud)?

I believe that megachurch pastor and author Rick Warren has the answer. *"True humility is not thinking less of yourself; it is thinking of yourself less."*[9] Not thinking less of yourself - be proud of what you are doing. But thinking of yourself less - be humble, be a servant, walk the talk, carry the water for your people.

Rule #2 for a fulfilling career: Be humble that you have this privilege.

Rule #3. Your career is an important part of who you are. There are many aspects making up who you really are - the genuine you. Your life. Your family. Your values. Your education. Your experiences. Your goals. Your god. These are all important.

Your career is also an important part of who you are. Theodore Roosevelt: *"Far and away the best prize that life offers is the chance to work hard at something worth doing."*[10] What you are doing is worth doing. Work hard at it.

Respect your career. Make the most of it. Fall in love with your job all over again, and then keep the romance alive.

Do not trivialize your career. Spend time learning. Get better at what you do every year. Share what you learn with others.

So that when you are ready to retire, you will to be able to say that your career was really important to you. It was a lot of work, you invested a lot of time, there was stress, there was frustration; yet, bottom line, there was joy, and there was fulfillment. It was worth it.

One more thing and here I quote Plato: *"Those having torches will pass them on to others."*[11] You want to live your career so that when it becomes time to retire, your torch will still be shining brightly and with pride and humility you can pass it on to others.

Rule #3 for a fulfilling career: Your career is an important part of who you are.

Rule #4. There is more to life than your career. You must never forget the balance - the balance between your work life and your personal life.

No one ever says on their deathbed, "I wish I had spent more time at the office (or clinic or hospital)." You people are committed. You people are driven. You, no doubt, already spend way too much time at the office. You need to be just as driven about spending time in your personal life, with your family, with your friends. If you have children, you don't want to end up saying, "I wish I had spent more time with my kids when they were growing up."

You must never forget the balance. Fill your life with breathtaking moments. You have heard the adage, *"Life is not measured by the number of breaths that you take, but rather by its breathtaking moments."*[12] When you think about it, there are not a whole lot of breathtaking moments at the clinic! The breathtaking moments have to do with family. With sharing love. With volunteer projects. With seeing the world. Don't sacrifice on behalf of your career the opportunities for breathtaking moments. I have heard that you only go around once.

You need to take time to reflect on this. You need to wrestle with your priorities. You need to plan how you will do this. Write out your plan. If you are married, share it with your spouse. Or better yet, develop it together with your spouse. Think seriously about sharing it with your boss. But you need to make it happen. And I guarantee you that it will not happen without a plan…and a commitment to making it work. Without a plan and a commitment you will be devoured by your career.

Two physicians who worked for me come to mind. One was quite proud that he had not taken a vacation day for three years. Devoured by his career. The other had just returned from being present at the start of the Iditarod dogsled race in Alaska. A breathtaking moment.

Your career is an important part of who you are. But never fail to heed Rule #4 for a fulfilling career: There is more to life than your career.

Rule #5. There are a lot of irritations; focus on what is important. It has been said that wisdom in leadership is the art of knowing what to overlook. How important this concept is. So many irritations - every day. Focus on what is really important. Overlook the unimportant.

Every day the frustrations and the irritations come along. There is always something not working right. You can burn up both your adrenaline and your arteries stressing over these everyday irritations. Or you can teach yourself to take a deep breath, smile, enjoy the irony of the frustration, and move on. Discipline yourself in the art of knowing what to overlook.

As a leader, save your energy for what is really important. When you get frustrated, ask yourself how important is this really in the scheme of things. How important is this in the lives of your patients? How important is this in the lives of your colleagues? How important is this to AltaMed? How important is this in relation to what you are ultimately trying to accomplish in your career – the desired results pillar of your leadership philosophy? Think about what is happening, decide what is really important, and then get irritated about that.

Some years ago during a session at the American College of Physician Executives I had the privilege of sitting at the feet of a very insightful young poet named David Whyte. One of the things he said which has stuck with me through the years is this: *"One of the disciplines for building a rich soul life is the simple act, on a daily basis, of remembering what is important to you."*[13] David Whyte was talking about a rich soul life. He could also have been talking about a rule for a fulfilling career - remembering on a daily basis what is important to you.

The other day I got out a can opener and was busy opening a can of worms when I thought, "What am I doing?" Focus on what is really important.

Rule #5 for a fulfilling career: There are a lot of irritations. Focus on what is important.

Rule #6. Affirm your colleagues and co-workers. Thank everybody. Everybody likes affirmation. Everybody needs affirmation. You occupy a very special and elite position at AltaMed. Other employees look up to you. An affirmation from you is profoundly meaningful. It will make someone's day - possibly even their week or month or year. Be lavish, but genuine, in your affirmations.

Isn't it interesting how much impact positive reinforcement and affirmation can have on our morale, our self-image, our ultimate happiness? An affirmation from you can change a life. Be lavish, but genuine, in your affirmations.

You also need to be lavish but genuine in your thank you's. Your thank you's should be continuous and highly visible.

Being thanked on a regular basis is listed as one of the major satisfiers for employees. You could not do what you are doing without the help of so many people - appointments, front desk, cashiers, medical assistants, nurses, lab, x-ray, managers, secretaries, and so many others. Take a minute and thank them. Make it your policy not to go home at night without first finding someone who has helped you and thanking her or him. If you can't find anyone in the immediate vicinity to thank, sit down at your computer and send an e-mail thank you to someone who labors on your behalf - maybe even to someone on the senior leadership team. Saying "thank you" to someone who has helped you that day may be the most important thing that you do all day.

Think about the approximate number of people with whom you work closely every day and upon whom you depend to get your job done. How many of these people have you thanked for helping you in the past week? For the most part, we are not very good at this.

Make a list of names of those who help you every day. Put a different name on your calendar for every day during a month. And do this month after month. On that day, go thank that person. It doesn't have to be for any particular task. It could just be, "I want you to know how much I appreciate all your help." Or "how much I appreciate all you do for our patients," or "for AltaMed."

By the way, have you ever received an unanticipated note of appreciation from a colleague? I have received an occasional one over the years. What did I do with the note when it arrived? I read it. I read it again. I put it aside for five minutes and then read it again. I put it in my monthly tickler file and read it once a month for the next year. I sent a copy to my mother! It really feels good to receive a note of appreciation when you are not expecting it.

There is so much power in appreciation, so much power in affirmation, and so much power in those two words, "thank you". Management guru Tom Peters, *"Most managers wildly underestimate the power of the tiniest personal touch."*[14] Every day make it a habit to share Tom Peter's "tiniest personal touch" with your colleagues and co-workers.

Rule #6 for a fulfilling career: Affirm your colleagues and coworkers. Thank everybody.

Rule #7. You are very fortunate. Pass it on. You know how fortunate you are. You have a good job. You are a member of a highly respected profession. You work for a highly regarded organization. You have food on your table. You have a pillow to lay your head on at night. You have family. You have friends. Many of you have kids. Accept and understand and appreciate your good fortune. And then pass it on.

Did you see the movie, "Pay It Forward" with Kevin Spacey, Helen Hunt, and Haley Joel Osment, who played Trevor McKinney? In the movie Trevor comes up with the idea of paying a favor not back, but forward--repaying good deeds with new good deeds done to three new people. Trevor's efforts to make good on his idea brought a revolution in the lives of an ever-widening circle of people completely unknown to him. Pay it forward. Pass it on.

Have you seen the bumper stickers, *"Practice random acts of kindness?"* Have you ever tried that? Totally random. Totally unsolicited. Pay for the car behind you at the toll booth. When in a long line trade your place with someone behind you. When eating breakfast at Waffle House, if you see two police officers in a booth across from you, pick up their check. Keep your eyes open for a chance to surprise someone with an act of kindness or generosity. If they thank you, tell them to pass it on.

On a daily practical level go out of your way to practice random acts of kindness to the support staff manning the low paying but important jobs at AltaMed. Never forget - there are no unimportant jobs, no unimportant people, and no unimportant acts of kindness. Every day they help you. Pass it on. Surprise them with a random act of kindness. Always remember the Tom Peters concept of the "power of the tiniest personal touch." Make their day. You will find that if you make someone's day, it will make your day also.

Winston Churchill is credited with saying it: *"You make a living by what you get. You make a life by what you give."*[15] Pass it on.

Whenever someone does something special for you, pass it on. Whenever your good fortune occurs to you, pass it on.

Rule #7 for a fulling career: You are very fortunate. Pass it on.

Rule #8. Take care of your patients, take care of each other, and take care.

Take care of your patients. I share with you now the words of physician and educator Francis Peabody, words with which he closed a lecture to Harvard medical students on October 21, 1925. These words have subsequently been burned indelibly into the minds of generations of medical students: *"The secret of the care of the patient is caring for the patient."*[16]

Never forget that the central focus is your patient. In spite of all the chaos and all the changes, and all the distractions, the central focus is your patient. Never forget, also, that every patient whom you encounter is in some way hurting. It might be a physical hurt. It might be a social hurt, or an emotional hurt, or even a spiritual hurt. But every patient is a human being who is, in some way, hurting. And you at AltaMed are in the business of the healing of human hurts.

Take care of your patients - with caring hands and loving hearts.

Take care of each other. What you do every day at AltaMed is so stressful and takes so much energy and determination. You can do it only by helping and supporting each other. You draw strength from each other. You must always remember, though, that you also are human. Your colleagues and co-workers are human. You are people helping people. Yet you are human just like your patients are human. You also have hurts. *Everyone you meet is fighting a battle you know nothing about.* Be sensitive to that.

We all need to be quicker to put our arms around each other and say:

"I know that what you do is very hard."
"I know that your life is not easy."
"I know that the stress in your job drains your energy."
"I know that you are hurting in some way."
"I am here to help our patients, but I am here to support you also."

Take care of each other.

Take care. Finally now, the time has come to say, "Take care." As a way of saying, "Take care", I want to share with you three personal reflections which have become meaningful to me over the years.

The first reflection is one I heard at a seminar led by Mike Vance. At the time Mike Vance was the Director of Creativity for Walt Disney. He was talking about life and the importance of making right decisions, the importance of focusing on values and the other meaningful things in life. The reflection was this: *"Life is too long not to do it right."*[17] We often hear that life is too short. But I thought his reflection was a profound insight. Life is too long not to do it right. We need to reflect on this in terms of the decisions that we make and the values that we establish.

The second reflection is attributed to Wilfred A. Peterson, *"Happiness doesn't always come from doing what we like to do, but rather from liking what we have to do."*[18] From time to time, and sometimes often, we find ourselves stuck with a project or a task, or even a job, which we don't enjoy and would rather not be doing. When that happens we need to remember that we can choose how we respond. We can choose to respond negatively with complaining and misery and low morale. Or we can choose to respond positively by being upbeat, hopeful, and determined to make the best of it. As Carlos Castenada, author and philosopher, has reminded us, *"We either can make ourselves miserable, or we can make ourselves strong. They both require the same amount of energy."*[19] And so, the second reflection becomes real: "Happiness can come from choosing to like what we have to do."

Reflection #3 comes from George Will. George Will is a well-known columnist and commentator. *"The point of life is not to be great, but rather to be all you can be."*[20] My wish for each one of you is that you become all that you can be. Some of you will become great, but that is not the point. The point of life is that you reach your fullest potential; that you become genuine, that you become real, and that you become all that you can be.

And so, rule #8 for a fulfilling career: Take care of your patients, take care of each other, and take care.

Let me close by sharing with you the wisdom of four giants in their respective fields - wisdom that encapsulates an all-encompassing bottom-line requirement for experiencing a fulfilling career. In thinking about leadership and in thinking about being human, each one of the four makes the case that there is a fundamental dynamic which must permeate each one of us, and which must permeate everything we do. And that dynamic for a fulfilling career - that bottom line - is love.

Eight Rules for a Fulfilling Career

Here are the four:

First, as leadership expert, James Autry, wrote in Love and Profit, the Art of Caring Leadership, *"Good management is largely a matter of love."*[21] Love must become the fundamental dynamic of our universe in health care. It is the focus that can make it all possible.

Second, Avedis Donabedian. In the late 20th century Dr. Donabedian was recognized as one of the true authorities on health care quality. This is what he said about the secret of quality. *"Ultimately the secret of quality is love. You have to love your patient. You have to love your profession. You have to love your God. If you have love, you can then work backward to monitor and improve the system."*[22]

Third, step with me for just a moment into the mind of the late French philosopher and theologian, Tielhard de Chardin, from his incredible book, The Phenomenon of Man.[23]

Someday, after mastering the winds and the waves and the tides and gravity, we shall harness - for God - the energies of love. And then, for the second time in the history of the world, man will have discovered fire.

I have one overarching message for you today, and it is that the ultimate secret for a fulfilling career is harnessing the energies of love. The rediscovery of fire, must become the essence of our life as leaders. Leadership without love is only a shell. Management without love is hollow. If we can harness the energies of love, we will rediscover fire.

Finally, Dr. Jack McConnell, distinguished physician, scientist and humanitarian. Dr. McConnell is retired now. His career was with Johnson and Johnson. His job title: Director of Advanced Technology. Johnson and Johnson told him to pursue whatever was of interest him. He led the team that invented Tylenol. He played a key role in the development of MRI technology. He was active in unlocking the secrets of DNA. Yet this genius of a physician scientist was a man with a huge heart full of compassion for the underserved. Upon retirement he founded a movement which has now spread across the country - Volunteers in Medicine, retired physicians providing health care for free to the poor.

I invited Dr. McConnell to speak to my staff. I wanted my staff to hear from this man, who had already changed the world, about compassion, and caring, and love for the underserved. When he finished his presentation, my staff gave him a standing ovation.

During the day Dr. McConnell was asked if he would comment on the meaning of life. He thought for a moment. I have never forgotten his answer.

Life is a web of love. Our role is not to break that web, but rather to make it stronger.[24]

The meaning of life: to strengthen the web of love. This has to be what our leadership is all about - demonstrating, strengthening, and living the web of love for each other and for our patients. The web of love becomes the foundation for building a fulfilling career.

Making a better world.

Let me close with one final story. Some years ago I was in Washington, D.C. for a meeting of the National Association of Community Health Centers. I needed to go to another part of the city, so I hailed a cab. The driver turned out to be an African-American grandmother who was one of the most warm, open, outgoing, friendly, caring, interested, and affirming human beings I have ever met. During that taxi ride, I learned all about her family and her children and her grandchildren. I learned about her philosophy of life and why she loved so much driving that taxi on the streets of Washington, D.C. And she learned all about my family and my children and my philosophy of life. She learned what I did in Indianapolis and why I loved doing that so much. It was a marvelously affirming time.

When we reached my destination, the taxi stopped, I paid her and got out. The last thing that she did was wave to me and say, "Have a great life!" Now most of us, when we are in a good mood, might say to someone, "Have a great day." She said, "Have a great life!" I felt, "Wow! That is beautiful!"

What I want to say to each of you, who everyday do so much to make this a better world, is simply this. "Have a great life!"

Chapter Twelve

Your Legacy Awaits

> This final lecture presents a clear challenge to think about your own legacy and what you truly want it to be. The task then becomes finding time for inner exploration - reflecting on what must be done to align reality with aspirations for your own legacy.

An Irish Blessing

May the road rise up to meet you.
May the wind be always at your back.
May the sun shine warm upon your face.
And the rains fall soft upon your fields.
And until we meet again,
May God hold you in the hollow of His hand.

Traditional Gaelic Blessing

Have you thought about what your legacy at AltaMed might be? Your legacy is what you leave behind. Every leader leaves a legacy. The stories people tell about you after you are gone. Your reputation. Your accomplishments. Your contributions. The way you were.

I would like to reflect for a few moments about legacies—in particular, your legacy and what you can and should be doing about it. What do you think your legacy might be?

Your Legacy Awaits

Your legacy is something that you hand down to those who come after you - whether in your personal and family life or here at AltaMed. It is your reputation, which you have constructed and which remains after you are gone.

We leave legacies in what we write. We leave legacies through our contributions. Most important, we leave legacies in who we are as human beings and how we are as colleagues, co-workers, and leaders.

Let us spend a few moments thinking about our individual legacies. Your legacy might be a major contribution which you made. It might be the impact you had on the culture of AltaMed or your own department. It might be your intensely personal values which were clear to everyone - integrity, gratitude, or something else. It might be your active participation in improvement activities. It might be your attitude.

According to management expert Les Wallace, the fact of the matter is that you are leaving a legacy whether you are thinking about it or not.[1] It could be positive. It might be negative. It could be nothing at all. You are contributing to your legacy every day.

And so, it is good to spend a bit of time thinking about your legacy. If you left AltaMed this week, what do you suspect your legacy might be? What would you like it to be? Are the two the same?

If you retired from AltaMed this week, what will people be saying about you and your contributions to AltaMed a month from now? Six months from now? What about you or your contributions to AltaMed would you like people to recognize after you leave?

What will your legacy be? What would you want it to be?

You need to take the time to think very deeply about the answer to each of these two questions. For the answers to these two questions will structure the way you live here at AltaMed.

To quote Les Wallace again, "*Great leaders take time for inner exploration and ask continually what their purpose in life might be, what they want to accomplish, and what they want to leave as their legacy.*"

The Leadership Lectures

"To be a great leader," Les says, *"you must take the time for inner exploration."*[1]

Inner exploration. I have never forgotten the commencement address from my college graduation. I don't remember the name of the speaker, but I do remember the subject. The title was, "Slow Down and Let Your Soul Catch Up."

Here now is my final thought to each of you regarding becoming an effective leader. Slow down and let your soul catch up. Find some time in your busy life for inner exploration. Find some time to slow down and let your soul catch up.

Life at AltaMed is not conducive to slowing down. Things seem to be speeding up more and more each day. It is easy to get caught up in the pressure and the rush. Too much to do. Too many deadlines. Too many fires to put out.

Never forget: To be a great leader, you have to make time to slow down and let your soul catch up.

> *Do you take the time for inner exploration?*
>
> *Have you spent time thinking about your personal leadership philosophy?*
>
> *Have you put together a career development plan?*
>
> *Have you thought about the one thing you could do that, if you did it consistently, would make a huge impact on your professional or your personal life?*
>
> *Have you started using a Harry Roberts "To Be" checklist?*
>
> *Are you thinking about what you want to accomplish at AltaMed?*
>
> *Are you thinking about what you want to accomplish in life?*
>
> *Are you thinking about what kind of leader you aspire to be?*
>
> *What do you want your legacy to be?*
>
> *Have you thought about what you have to do to get there?*

The most important thing that you can do to become an effective leader and to enhance your legacy is to find the time in your busy and chaotic life for Les Wallace's inner exploration. You can make the time if it is important enough to you. One lunch hour each week isolate yourself and think about these questions. Or set your alarm for 15-20 minutes early every day and use those extra minutes for inner exploration. Or take a day off and go to the beach and sit in the sand and let your soul catch up. You can figure out a plan that will work for you.

You have to know yourself. You have to know who you want to be. You have to know what you want to become. You must slow down and let your soul catch up.

Remember this: *It is never too late to become what you want to be.*[2] It is never too late to be what you might have been. But you will never get there if you do not step off the treadmill occasionally and sit down and think about these things. The importance of inner exploration.

Slow down and let your soul catch up.

Your legacy awaits you.

And until we meet again,
May God hold you in the hollow of His hand.

Bibliography

Chapter One: Leadership and the Rediscovery of Fire
1. Welch MB . www.alllpoetry.com. 1921.
2. Autry J. *Love and Profit, the Art of Caring Leadership*. Harper Collins, 1992.
3. Teilard de Chardin P. *The Phenomenon of Man*. Harper and Row, 1959.
4. Mullin F. "Founder of Quality Assessment Encounters a Troubled System Firsthand." *Health Affairs*. 20(1) 137-141, January 2001.
5. Disney R. www.values.com
6. Kaiser L. President of Kaiser and Associates. Brighton, Colorado. Notes from various ACPE lectures.
7. Huey J. The new post-heroic leadership. *Fortune*, 129, 42-50, 1994
8. McConnell J. Personal communication.
9. Covey S. *The Seven Habits of Highly Effective People*. Simon & Schuster, 1989.
10. Belasco J and Stayer R. *Flight of the Buffalo*. Warner Books, 1993, pg. 7.
11. The Certifying Commission in Medical Management. An Affiliate of the American Association for Physician Leadership, 2017.
12. Hoffer E. *The Passionate State of Mind and Other Aphorisms*. Hopewell Publications, 1955.
13. Hugo V. *Les Miserables*. Preface. The Heritage Press, 1938.

Chapter Two: The Five Fundamental Tasks of a Transformational Leader
1. Silverstein S. *Where the Sidewalk Ends*. Harper Collins Publishers, 1974.
2. Kettering C. *Charles Kettering Quotes*. www.brainyquotes.com.
3. Bennis W and Nanus B. *Leaders: Strategies for Taking Charge*. Harper and Row, 1986.
4. Wallace L. *Les Wallace-Handout-Personal-Success*. Pdf. www.mana.us. 2014.
5. Kaiser L. The Kaiser Institute. Brighton, Colorado.

Bibliography

6. Bennis, W. *An Invented Life: Reflection on Leadership and Change.* Basic Books, 1994.
7. Collins J and Poras J. *Built to Last: Successful Habits of Visionary Companies.* Harper Business Essentials, 2004.
8. Kotter JP. "What Leaders Really Do." *Harvard Business Review*, December 2001.
9. Kouzes J and Posner B. *The Leadership Challenge.* John Wiley and Sons, 2002.
10. Maggio R. *How to Say It.* Third Edition. Prentice Hall Press, 2009.

Chapter Three: Building the Mental Model for Leadership

1. Prelutsky J. *Kaleidoscope Anthology Two.* Ginn and Company, 2004, pg 32.
2. Benson D. *Breathtaking Moments.* "Thought for the day Collection." Blurb.com. 2010, pg 330.
3. Shuman B. *Beyond the Library of the Future.* Libraries Unlimited, 1997, pg 160.
4. Bennis W. *The Invented Life. Reflections on Leadership and Change.* Basic Books: The Perseus Books Group, 1994, pg. 106.
5. Kotter JP. *A Force for Change: How Leadership Differs From Management.* The Free Press, Simon and Schuster, 1990.
6. Wallace L. *A Legacy of 21st Century Leadership. A Guide for Creating a Climate of Leadership Throughout Your Organization.* iVerse Publications, 2007.

Chapter Four: Crafting Your Personal Leadership Philosophy

1. Wilcox EW. *The Best Loved Poems of the American People.* Doubleday Publishing Group, 1936.
2. Covey S. *The 7 Habits of Highly Effective People.* Simon & Schuster, 1989, Pg. 98.

Chapter Five: Leading Beyond the Bottom Line

1. Adapted from *Dreams in Homespun*, a volume of poems of Sam Walter Foss, published by Lothrop, Lee and Shepard Company of New York. Copyright 1897 by Lee and Shepherd and 1925 by Carrie M. Conant Foss.

2. Schenke R., Gaintner JR., Hickey ME, Hodge RH., Ludden JW., Randolph LM. *Physician Executive*. July-August 2000, pp 6-11.
3. Lauer C. *Southwest Airlines*. ABC-Clio, 2010, Page 111.
4. Oakley E., Krug D. *Enlightened Leadership: Getting to the Heart of Change*. Simon & Schuster, 1994.
5. Ryan E. Developer of *Hiring the Best System*. Briefings Publishing Group. Quoted by Giesener, J. "Hiring the wrong people costs you three times their annual sales," *Linked In*. March 3, 2015.
6. Data from the Container Store website. "Our employee first culture." www.containerstore.com.
7. Tindell K., Schilling C. *Uncontainable*. Hatchette Book Group, 2014.
8. Lampton B. "My Pleasure—the Ritz-Carlton Hotel." *Expert Magazine*, Vol. 3, Issue 6, 2003.
9. Crane M. "To Train or Not to Train." *Forbes*, December 4, 2006.
10. Thomas J., Sassen E. "Why Satisfied Customers Defect." *Harvard Business Review*, Nov/Dec 1995.
11. Evans M. *George Elliott Quotes*. www.values.com.
12. "Starbucks' Six Guiding Principles". *Living Our Values*. Corporate Social Responsibility. Fiscal 2003 Annual Report.
13. Hoffman J. "Secrets of Ritz Carlton's Legendary Customer Service." *PSA Perspective*, May 8, 2014.
14. Fingar P. *Extreme Competition*. Meghan-Kiffer Press, 2006.
15. Shaw C. "Fifteen Statistics That Should Change the Business World – But Haven't." *Linked-In*. June 2013.
16. Wilson J. "Employee indifference makes a difference." www.vistage.com. August 5, 2014.
17. Baker R. *Pricing on Purpose. Creating and Capturing Value*. John Wiley and Sons, 2006, Page 165.
18. Morris T. www.business2community.com. March 2016.

Chapter Six: Embracing Change: Four Critical Concepts
1. Silverstein S. *Where the Sidewalk Ends*. Harper and Row, 1974.
2. Kaiser L. President of Kaiser and Associates. Brighton, Colorado. Notes from various ACPE lectures.
3. Huey J. "The New Post-Heroic Leadership." *Fortune*, February 21, 1994.

Bibliography

4. Peters T. Author and consultant on business management practices. Best known for *In Search of Excellence* (co-authored with Robert Waterman.)
5. Gibson R. *Rethinking the Future*. Forward by Alvin Tofler. Nicholas Brealey Publishing, 1996.
6. Vance M . Former Dean of Disney University and co-founder of Creative Thinking Association of America. Personal notes from a presentation at a meeting of the American College of Physician Executives.
7. Belasco J and Stayer R. *Flight of the Buffalo*. Warner Books, Inc. 1993, Pg.88.
8. Ford H. *Henry Ford Quotes*. www.goodreads.com.
9. Belasco J and Stayer R. *Flight of the Buffalo*. Warner Books, Inc. 1993, Pg.41.
10. Labovitz G, Rosansky,V and Varian T. *Leadership: Taking Charge of Change*. Organizational Dynamics, 1994.
11. Benson D. *Breathtaking Moments*. "Thought for the Day Collection." Blurb.com. 2010, Pg 345.
12. Robbins T. *Tony Robbins Quotes*. www.goodreads.com.
13. Palmer P. *Let Your Life Speak*. From Chapter Five, "Leading From Within." Jossey-Bass, 2000.

Chapter Seven: How to be Effective When There Is No Time

1. Guest E. *Collected Verse of Edward Guest*. Buccaneer Books, 1976.
2. Covey S. *The 7 Habits of Highly Effective People*. Simon & Schuster, 1989, Pg. 146.
3. Covey S, Merrill R, Merrill R. *First Things First*. New York, NY: Simon & Schuster, 1994. Pg. 32.
4. Covey S, Merrill R, Merrill R. *First Things First*. Simon & Schuster, 1994, Pg.75.
5. Covey S. *The 7 Habits of Highly Effective People*. Simon & Schuster, 1989, pp. 151-162.
6. Covey S. *The Seven Habits Study Guide. 3.1 Time Management*. www.en.wikibooks.org.
7. Ford H. *Henry Ford Quotes*. www.goodreads.com.

8. Covey S. *The 7 Habits of Highly Effective People.* Simon & Schuster, 1989, Pgs. 148.
9. Covey S. *The 7 Habits of Highly Effective People.* Simon & Schuster, 1989, Pg.146.
10. Covey S, Merrill R, Merrill R. *First Things First.* Simon & Schuster, 1994, Pg.88.
11. Covey S, Merrill R, Merrill R. *First Things First.* Simon & Schuster, 1994, Pg.102.
12. Roberts H. "Using Personal Checklists to Facilitate Total Quality Management." *The University of Chicago, Graduate School of Business.* Selected Paper Number 73.
13. Roberts H. and Sergesketter R. *Quality is Personal. A Foundation for Total Quality Management.* The Free Press. A Division of Simon & Schuster, 1993.
14. Covey S. *The 7 Habits of Highly Effective People.* Simon & Schuster, 1989, Pg.287.
15. Covey S. *The 7 Habits of Highly Effective People.* Simon & Schuster, 1989, Pg.289.
16. McKay D. *David O. McKay Quotes.* www.gooddreads.com.
17. Covey S. *The 7 Habits of Highly Effective People.* Simon & Schuster, 1989, Pg.295.
18. Emerson RW. *Ralph Waldo Emerson Quotes.* www.goodreads.com.
19. Durant W. *Will Durant Quotes.* www.brainyquote.com.

Chapter Eight: Twelve Tips for Leadership Effectiveness

1. Guest EA. *Collected Verse of Edgar Albert Guest.* Buccaneer Books, 1976.
2. Roberts H. "Using personal checklists to facilitate total quality management." *Selected Pages, Number 73. The University of Chicago, Graduate School of Business.*
3. Roberts H. *Quality is Personal: A Foundation for Total Quality Management.* Simon & Schuster, May 2010, Page 324.
4. Pinchot G & Pinchot E. *The Intelligent Organization: the Seven Essentials of Organizational Intelligence.* Barrett-Koehler Publishers, 1994, Page 65.

Bibliography

5. Edinger S. "If you want to communicate better, read this." *Forbes*, March 20, 2013.
6. Barna G. *Master Leaders: Revealing Conversations with Thirty Leadership Greats*. Tyndale House Publishers, 2009, Page 75.
7. Maxwell J. *The Five Levels of Leadership: Proven Steps to Maximize Your Potential*. Hachette Book Group, 2011.
8. Ilgaz Z. "Conflict Resolution: When Should Leaders Step In?" *Forbes*, May 15, 2014.

Chapter Nine: Connecting the Threads
1. Autry J. From "Threads", as found in the book, *Love and Profit: the Art of Caring Leadership*. Avon Books, 1991, pg. 32.
2. Covey S. *The 7 Habits of Highly Effective People*. Simon & Schuster, 1989, Pg. 95.
3. Werner E. Author and lecturer on leadership theory and practice. www.wermererhard.com.
4. Kotter JP. *A Force for Change. How Leadership Differs from Management*. The Free Press, Simon and Schuster, 1990, Chapter four.

Chapter Ten: Step Into It!
1. Hoffer E. *The Passionate State of Mind and Other Aphorisms*. Hopewell Publications, 1955.
2. From the 1936 movie *Swing Time*, lyrics by Dorothy Fields.
3. Palmer P. *Let Your Life Speak*. From Chapter Five, "Leading From Within." Jossey-Bass, 2000.
4. Bard C. *Carl Bard Quotes*. www.quoteland.com.

Chapter Eleven: Eight Rules for a Fulfilling Career
1. Andersen M. "*Leadership*." www.empoweredbypierce.com/the-lonely-place-of-leadership, 1970.
2. Peters T. *Tom Peters Quotes*. www.azquotes.com.
3. Covey S. *The Seven Habits of Highly Effective People*. Simon & Schuster, 1989.
4. Holmes O. Associate Justice, U. S. Supreme Court. www.values.com.
5. Zadre D. *Everyone Leads*. Compendium Publishing, 2006, pg. 20.

6. Ruskin J. *John Ruskin Quotes*. www.values.com.
7. Zadre D. *Everyone Leads*. Compendium Publishing, 2006, pg 88.
8. Briggs J. www.goodreads.com.
9. Warren R. *The Purpose Driven Life*. Zondervan Publishing, 2012.
10. Roosevelt T. *Theodore Roosevelt Quotes*. www.brainyquote.com,
11. Plato. *Plato Quotes*. www.azquotes.com.
12. Goodreads Library Group. www.goodreads.com.
13. Whyte D. Author's notes from a lecture at the American College of Physician Executives.
14. Benson D. "Thought for the Day Collection." *Breathtaking Moments*. Blurb, 2010, pg 350.
15. Churchill W. *Winston Churchill Quotes*. www.values.com.
16. Peabody F. "The Care of the Patient." *Journal of the American Medical Association*, 1927;88(12):877-882.
17. Vance M. Author's notes from a lecture at the American College of Physician Executives.
18. Peterson W. *Wilfred Peterson Quotes*. www.goodreads.com.
19. Zadre D. *Everyone Leads*. Compendium Publishing, 2006, pg 72.
20. Benson D." Thought for the Day Collection." *Breathtaking Moments*. Blurb.com. 2010, pg 349.
21. Autry J. *Love and Profit, the Art of Caring Leadership*. Harper Collins, 1992.
22. Mullin F. "A founder of quality assessment encounters a troubled system firsthand." *Health Affairs*, 20(1)137-41, Jan 2001.
23. Teilard de Chardin P. *The Phenomenon of Man*. Harper and Row, 1959.
24. McConnell, J. Personal communication.

Chapter Twelve: Your Legacy Awaits
1. Wallace L and Trinka J. *A Legacy of 21st Century Leadership*. iUniverse Press, 2007.
2. Evans MA. *George Eliot Quotes*. www.values.com.

About the Author

DALE S. BENSON, MD, CPE, FAAPL

Dale S. Benson, MD, CPE, FAAPL, family physician and physician executive, most recently served as Vice President of Innovation, Quality, and Practice Management and Director of the Leadership Development Institute for AltaMed Health Services in Los Angeles.

In 1969, Dale founded and for 30 years served as the Executive Director of the HealthNet Community Health Centers in Indianapolis. Immediately prior to joining AltaMed, he served as Vice President, Physician Practice Management and Vice President of Ambulatory Care for the Mercy Health System in Chicago.

He is certified as a Physician Executive (CPE) by the Certifying Commission in Medical Management and is a Distinguished Fellow of the American Association for Physician Leadership (FAAPL). For 12 years, he was also a field consultant and surveyor for The Joint Commission.

In 1987 Dale co-authored the Joint Commission book Quality Assurance in Ambulatory Care, as well as the 1990 Jossey-Bass book Excellence in Ambulatory Care. In 1992 he authored Measuring Outcomes in Ambulatory Care, published by the American Hospital Publishing Company. He has written and lectured extensively in the areas of leadership, quality, and efficiency in the ambulatory setting. He has taught more than 80 one and two day seminars on managing quality.

He has been a member of the Board of Directors of the American College of Physician Executives (now the American Association for Physician Leadership), and served as the President of the College. He has also served as Chair of the Certifying Commission in Medical Management.

Dale was presented the President's Award by the Society of Ambulatory Care Professionals in 1992 for contributions to understanding outcomes in the field of ambulatory care. In 1999, he received a Lifetime Achievement Award from the National Association of Community Health Centers, and the Sagamore of the Wabash Award from the Governor of Indiana (Indiana's highest honor for service to its citizens).

350 N. Meridian Street
Unit #303
Indianapolis, IN 46204
317-638-0075
dalebenson@sbcglobal.net

Made in the USA
Columbia, SC
08 April 2019